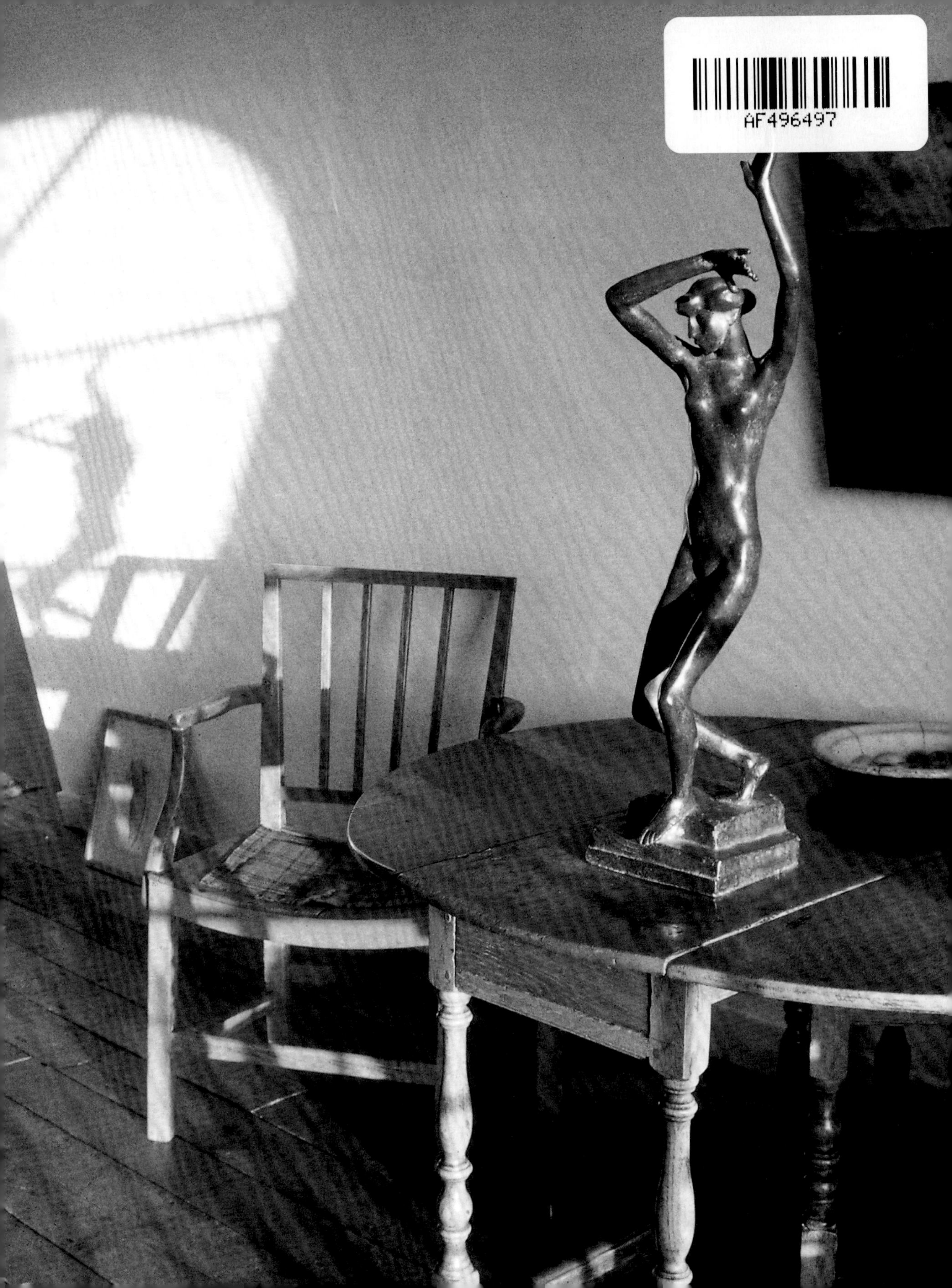
AF496497

NEW RHYTHMS
Henri Gaudier-Brzeska: Art, Dance and Movement in London 1911–15

Edited by Jennifer Powell

KETTLE'S YARD

NEW RHYTHMS
Henri Gaudier-Brzeska:
Art, Dance and Movement
in London 1911–15

Published by Kettle's Yard
University of Cambridge

Edited by Dr. Jennifer Powell
Copyedited by Christopher Connor
Picture research by Marie-France Kittler

Design by A Practice for Everyday Life
Produced, printed and bound by
DZA Druckerei zu Altenburg GmbH,
Germany (in an edition of 1200 copies)

ISBN 978-1-904561-51-4

© Kettle's Yard and the authors, 2015

Exhibition

17 March – 21 June 2015
Kettle's Yard
University of Cambridge

A selection of works touring to Harewood House,
Leeds, 11 July – 1 November 2015

Curated by Dr. Jennifer Powell
Assisted by Marie-France Kittler
and Guy Haywood

Kettle's Yard
Castle Street
Cambridge CB3 0AQ
United Kingdom
+44 (0)1223 748 100
www.kettlesyard.co.uk

Director: Andrew Nairne
Chair: Anne Lonsdale CBE

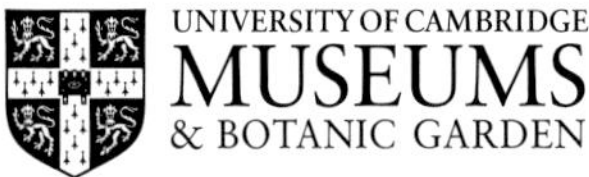

Support

Kettle's Yard relies on the generosity of
supporters to care for the collection and
historic buildings, and enable us to offer a
full programme of activities, from exhibitions,
learning activities and music to publications
and research. All gifts, large and small, help to
safeguard the collection for future generations,
and enable others to enjoy Kettle's Yard now
and in the future.

There are a variety of ways in which you can
help support Kettle's Yard and also benefit as
a UK or US taxpayer. For information please
visit www.kettlesyard.co.uk/supporters

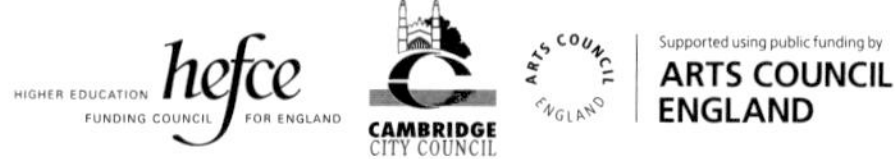

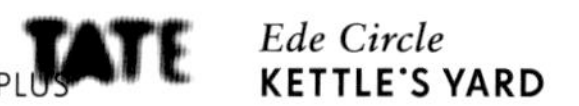

This exhibition has been generously supported
by the Henry Moore Foundation

The Henry Moore Foundation

StaticShield glazing for *Black & White poster
(aka Boxers)* by Tru Vue, supplied by Wessex
Pictures. TRU VUE

Dust-jacket front
Typeface design by A Practice for Everyday Life
(HGB Super Grotesk)

Dust-jacket back
Dancer (study), 1914, black ink on paper, Centre Pompidou, Paris

Inside page
View of *The Dancer*, Kettle's Yard House, Cambridge,
photograph by Paul Allitt

p. 7
fig. 1: Walter Benington, *Portrait of Henri Gaudier-Brzeska*, 1914,
photograph, silver print AMC 04892, Private Collection courtesy
Archive of Modern Conflict

p. 122
fig. 32: Jim Ede standing next to *Bird swallowing a Fish*, 1972,
photograph, Kettle's Yard Collection

p. 127
fig. 33: Walter Benington, *Portrait of Henri Gaudier-Brzeska*, 1914,
photograph, silver print AMC 04892, Private Collection courtesy
Archive of Modern Conflict

Back page
View of *Red Stone Dancer*, Kettle's Yard House, Cambridge,
photograph by Paul Allitt

Contents

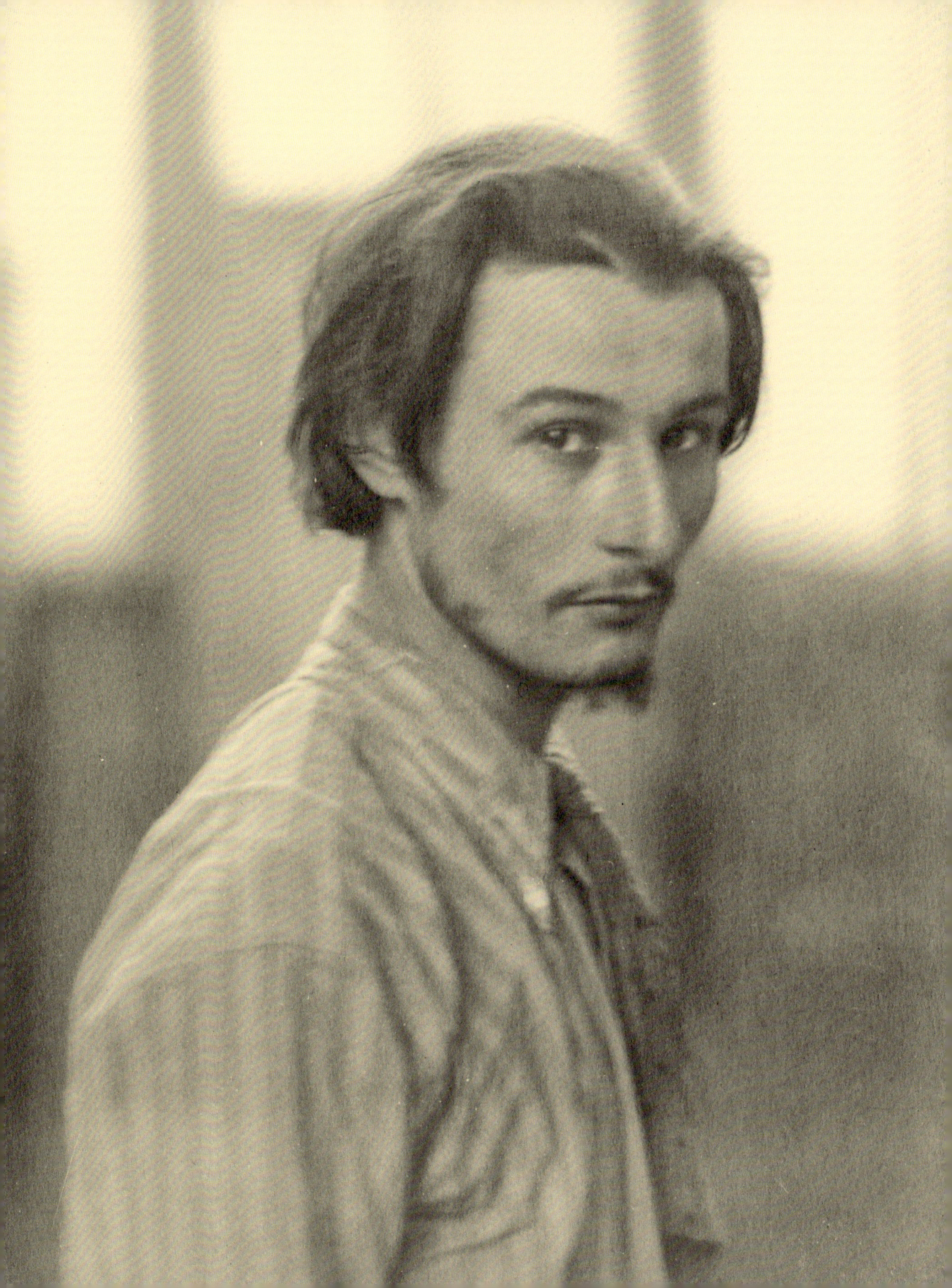

Foreword

Andrew Nairne

Henri Gaudier was born in 1891 in St. Jean de Braye, near to Orléans, south-west of Paris. He was killed in action on the 5 of June 1915, aged twenty-three, near Arras at Neuville-Saint-Vaast. His grave, in the huge war cemetery at La Targette, reads 'Gaudier Henri Alphonse, Sergent, Mort Pour La France'. In his memoir of Gaudier, the poet Ezra Pound wrote:

'A great spirit has been amongst us, and a great artist has gone'.

H. S. (Jim) Ede, later to become the creator of Kettle's Yard, was also fighting in the trenches in 1915, returning to England the following year suffering from nervous exhaustion. A decade later, while working as a curator at the Tate Gallery, the discovery of Gaudier's work marked a turning point in Ede's life. After acquiring the majority of the artist's estate in 1927, Ede did all in his power to champion his work most notably by writing a biography (first published in 1930) and later through the opening of Kettle's Yard itself. Kettle's Yard is home to one of the largest collections of drawings and sculptures by Gaudier. Despite living and working in London as an artist for barely four years from 1911 to 1914, Gaudier is now recognised as a pioneer of modern sculpture. Henry Moore was to note: 'Gaudier's writings and sculpture meant an enormous amount – they [...] were a confirmation to me as a young person that everything was possible'.

Ede's biography (originally titled *A Life of Henri Gaudier-Brzeska* and then given a new title *Savage Messiah* in 1931 and for subsequent editions) became a best seller, with novelist Rebecca West describing it on publication as 'one of the most interesting books about an artist ever written'. It is still in print. Believing his readers would know Ezra Pound's earlier memoir (1916), Ede focused on Gaudier's letters to his partner Sophie Brzeska (whose name he added to his own in 1911) and her own diaries, rather than a discussion of individual sculptures. The artist's letters offer a remarkable insight into his art, interests and ambition, while also revealing his intimate and sometimes tempestuous relationship with Sophie. In *Savage Messiah* Ede presents the life and art of Gaudier as inextricable; a way of viewing the world that was to be fundamental to the making and philosophy of Kettle's Yard.

NEW RHYTHMS Henri Gaudier-Brzeska: Art, Movement and Dance 1911–15 marks the centenary of Henri Gaudier-Brzeska's death. It celebrates an extraordinary artist's talent whose sculptures and drawings continue to be resonant and vital in the twenty-first century. Curated by Dr Jennifer Powell, it is the first exhibition to explore in depth the artist's relationship to movement and dance. As part of the exhibition we have commissioned a new work from composer Kate Whitley and choreographer Malgorzata Dzierzon, in collaboration with filmmaker David McCormick. Their work aims to inspire us to consider how Gaudier's works can be a catalyst for 'new rhythms' today.

We are delighted that a smaller edition of the exhibition will be presented at Harewood House in Yorkshire from July to November: our thanks to Lord and Lady Harewood and to Anna Dewsnap, Head of Collections and Nicola Stephenson, Exhibitions and Projects Producer.

An exhibition of this nature relies on the assistance, expertise and good will of many people. The exhibition has only been possible as a result of the generosity of our lenders, both public and private. Our sincere gratitude to the Archive of Modern Conflict; British Museum; Centre Pompidou; Fitzwilliam Museum, University of Cambridge; Jennings Fine Art; Lord and Lady Harewood; Saarland Museum; The Sherwin Collection; Bowman Sculpture Gallery; St James's Art Books; Tate; Albert Sloman Library, University of Essex; Syndics of Cambridge University Library; Victoria and Albert Museum and to those who wish to remain anonymous.

We are delighted to be publishing this new book alongside the exhibition. Thank you to the authors Dr Doïna Lemny, Dr Evelyn Silber and Dr Sarah Victoria Turner for their thought provoking essays and to the designers,

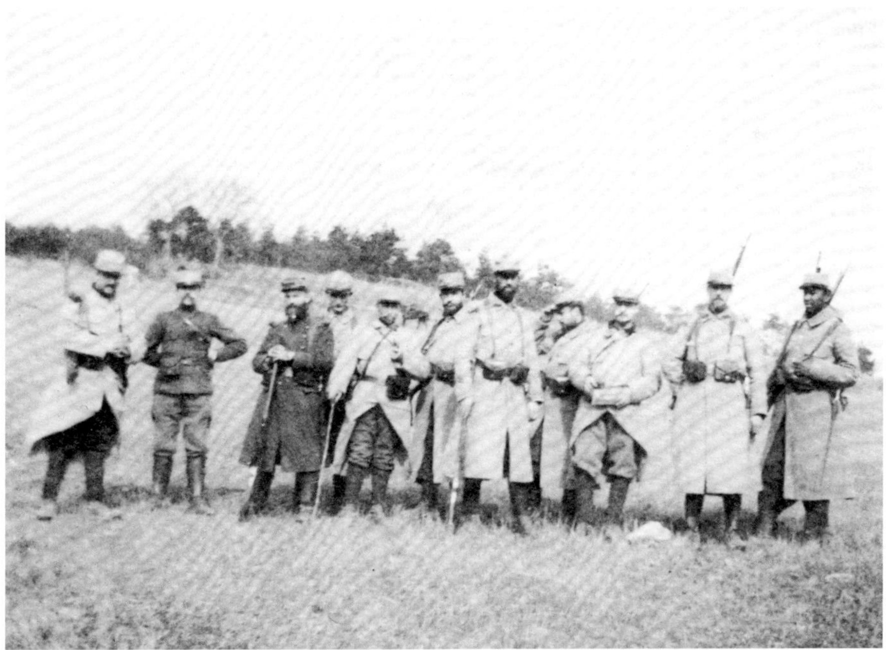

fig. 3
Henri Gaudier-Brzeska, fourth from left among
fellow soldiers at war, 1915, sepia, photograph, Tate

A Practice for Everyday Life. Many artists' estates and institutions have been generous in enabling us to reproduce works including: Ben Uri Gallery, Bristol Museum and Art Gallery, Leeds Museums and Galleries (Henry Moore Institute Archive), Modernist Journals Project, Musée Historique et Archéologique de l'Orléanais, Smart Museum of Art / The University of Chicago, and the William Roberts Society. We are also grateful to Adrian Locke, André Zlattinger (Christie's, London) and Stuart Lochhead (Daniel Katz Limited). In researching and preparing the exhibition and publication Dr Jon Wood, Scott Wilcox, Dr Jane Pritchard and Dr Evelyn Silber have been exceptionally supportive with their expertise and advice.

The Kettle's Yard team has come together to support this celebration of Gaudier's art. They have been superbly led by Senior Curator Dr Jennifer Powell, who has also edited this publication. Marie-France Kittler has worked tirelessly as Assistant Curator and further support has come from Guy Haywood, Susie Biller, Lucy Wheeler, Frieda Midgley and Laura Pryke. Kettle's Yard is enormously grateful to the Henry Moore Foundation for their support for this ambitious project. We are also indebted to our Ede Circle supporters, the Friends of Kettle's Yard and Arts Council England.

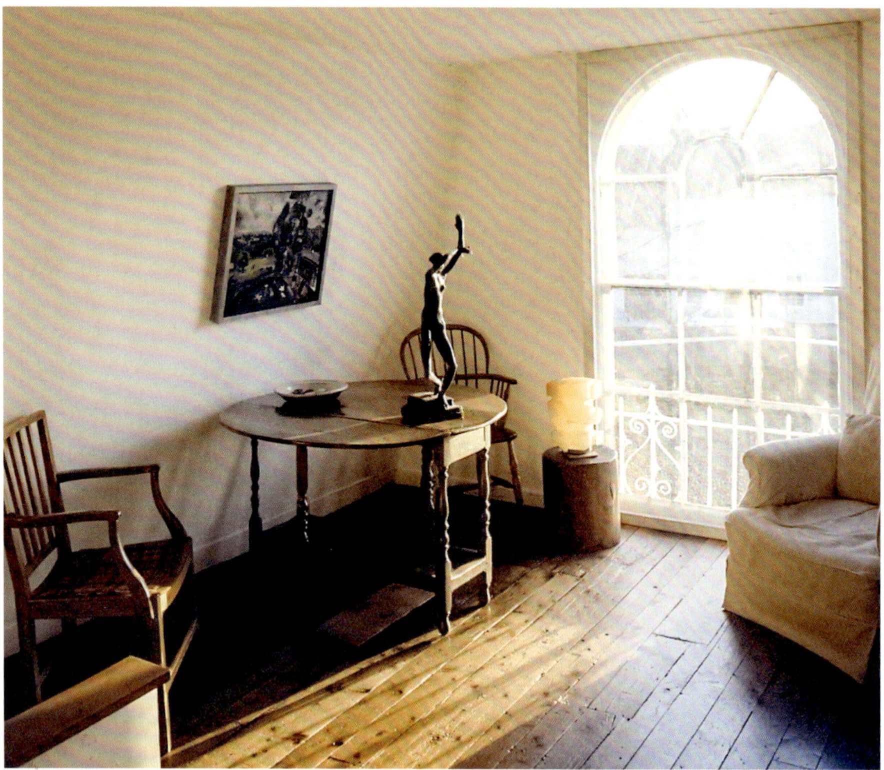

fig. 4
View of *The Dancer*, 1913, Kettle's Yard House, Cambridge

1
*Self Portrait with
a pipe (1)*, 1913

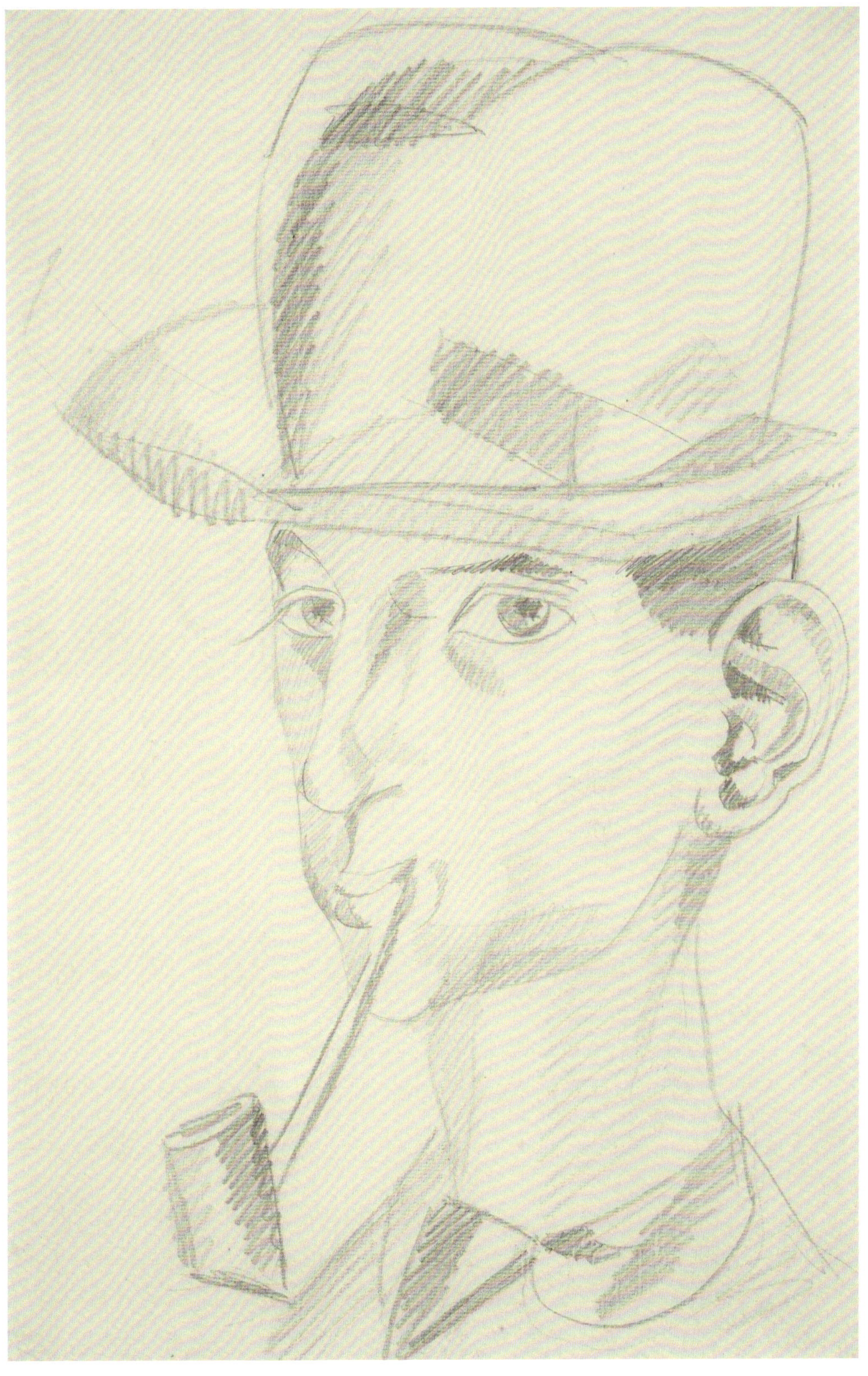

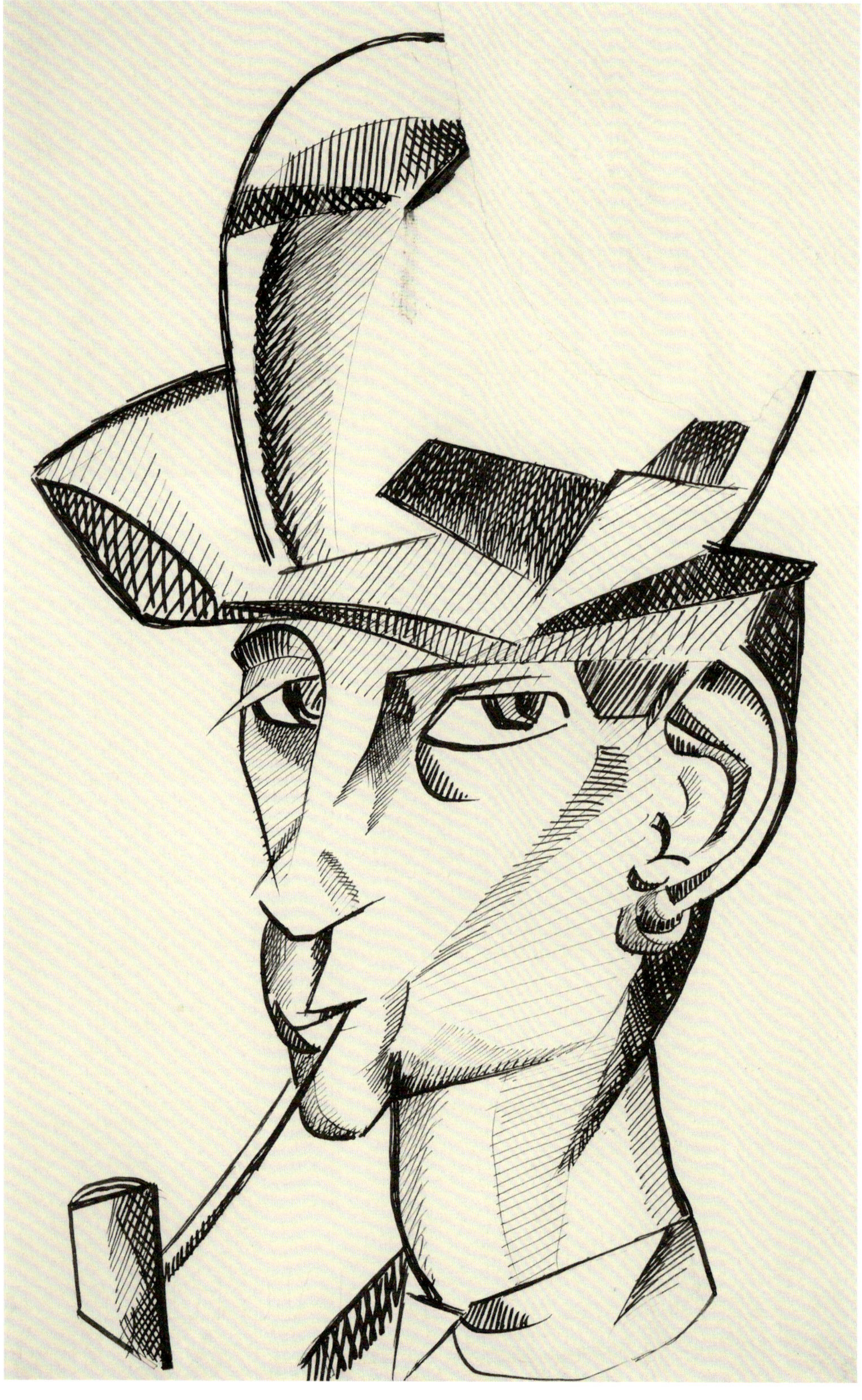

3
*Self Portrait with
a pipe (3)*, 1913

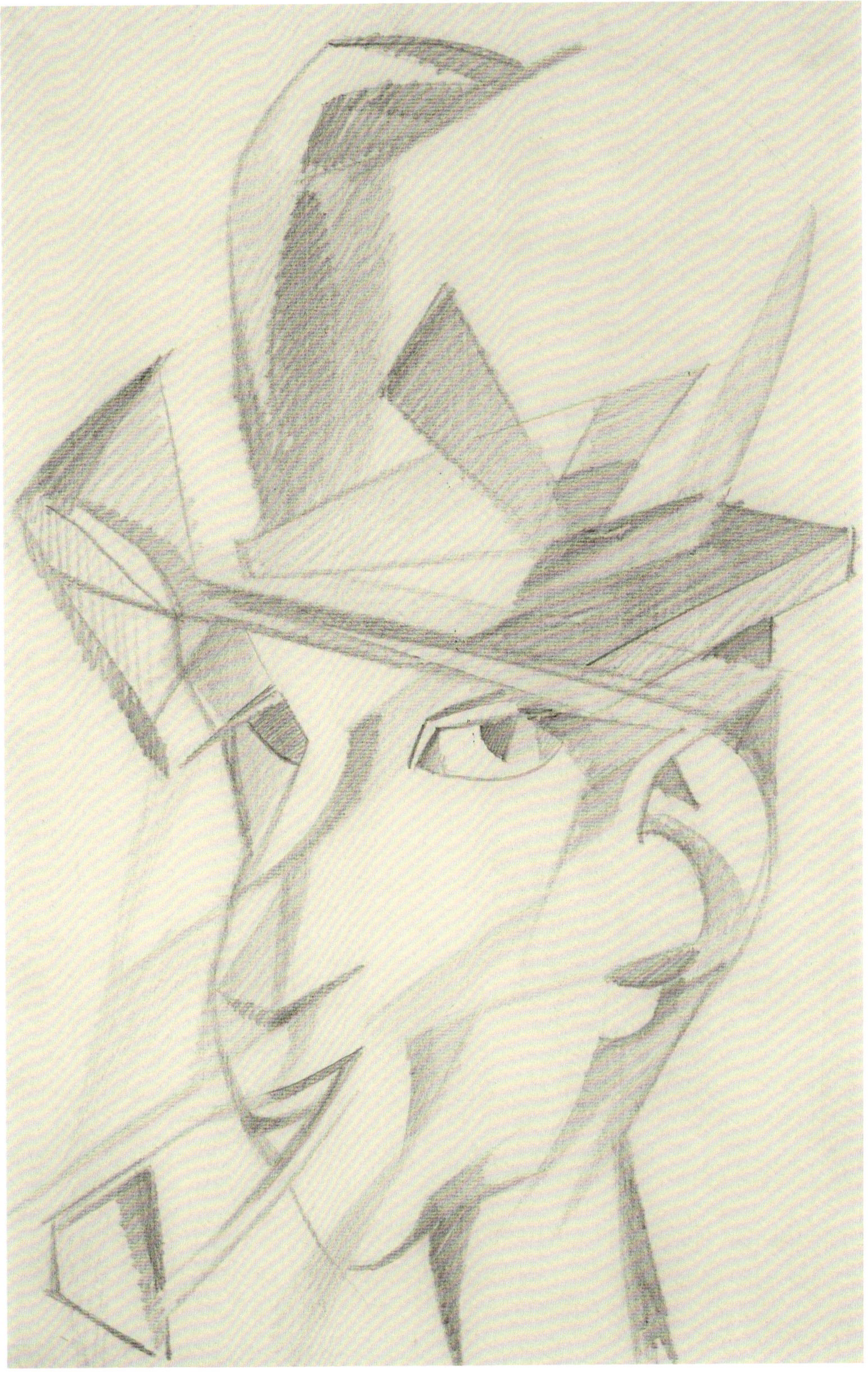

'Movement is the translation of life, and
if art depicts life, movement should come
into art, since we are only aware of life
because it moves.'

— Gaudier writing to Sophie Brzeska, 28 November 1912

THE DANCERS

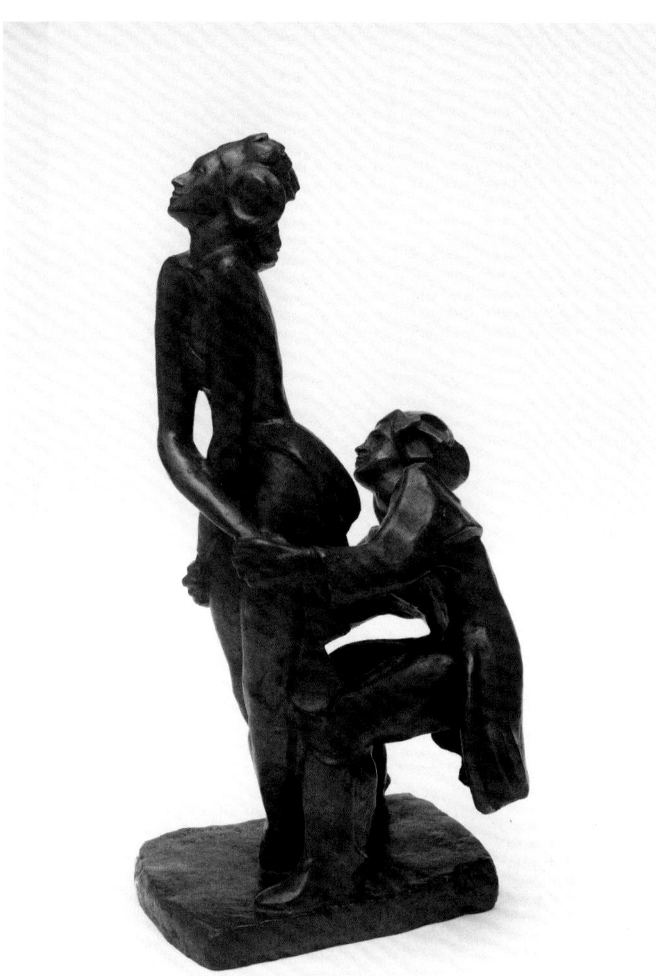

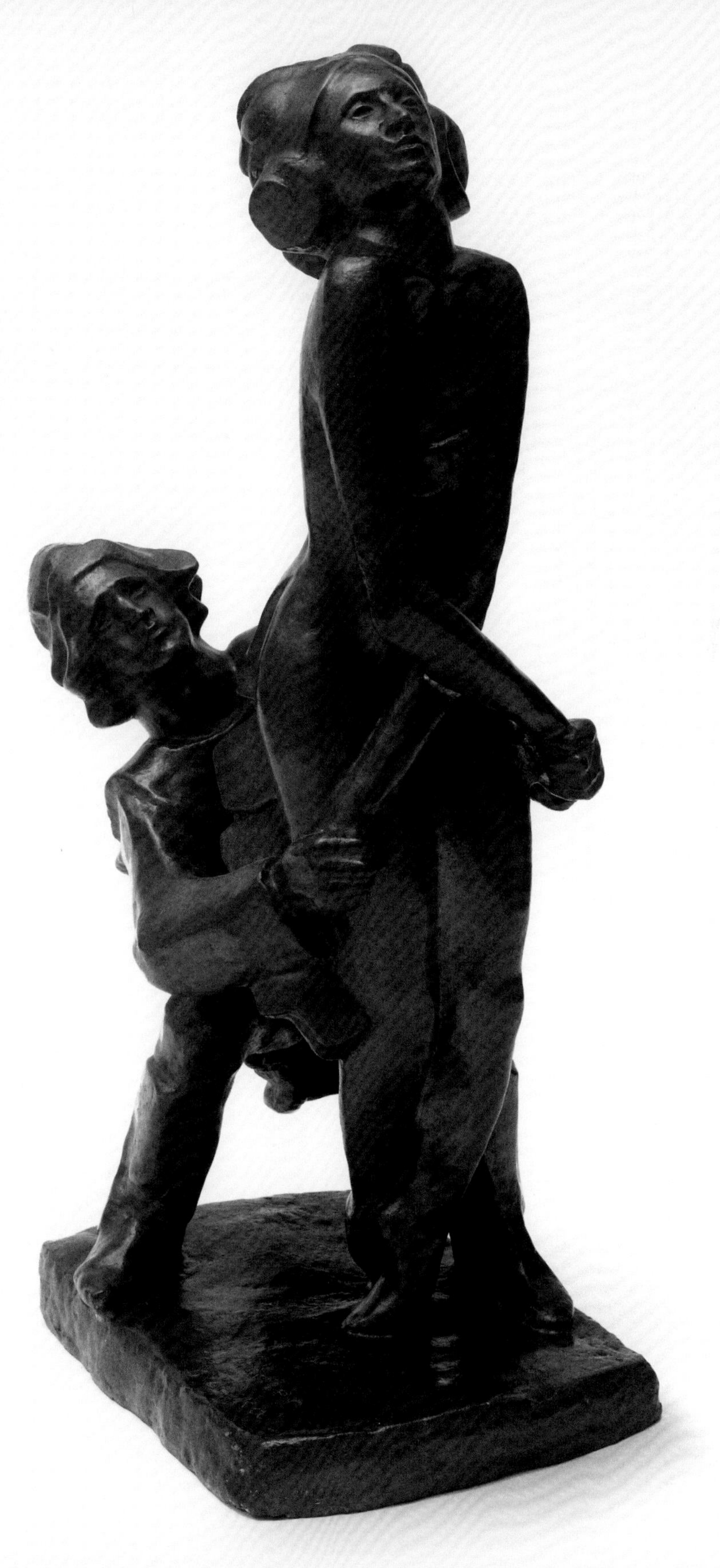

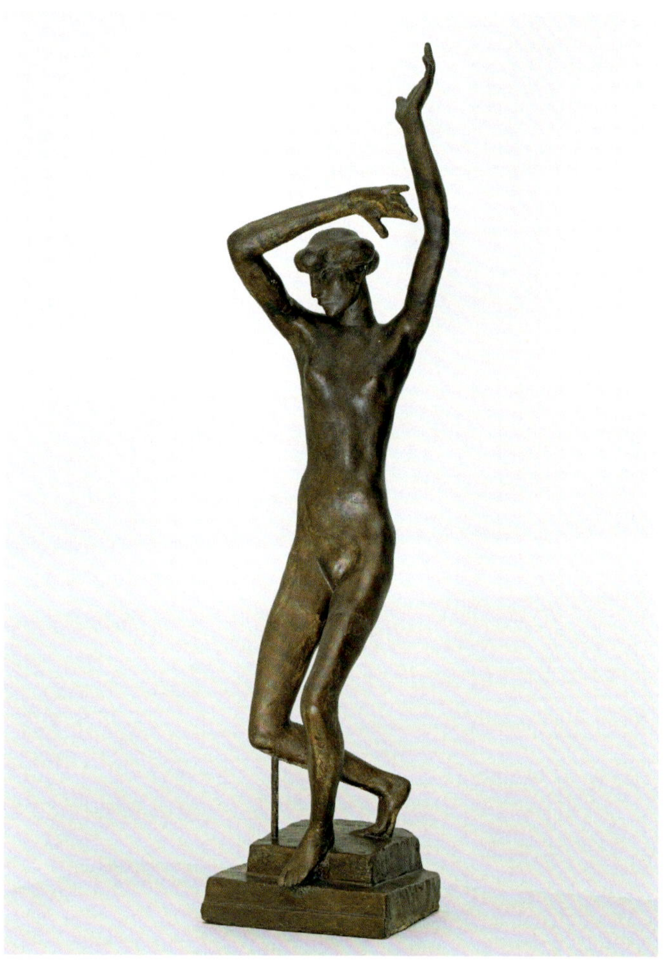

6
The Dancer, 1913
original plaster, Tate

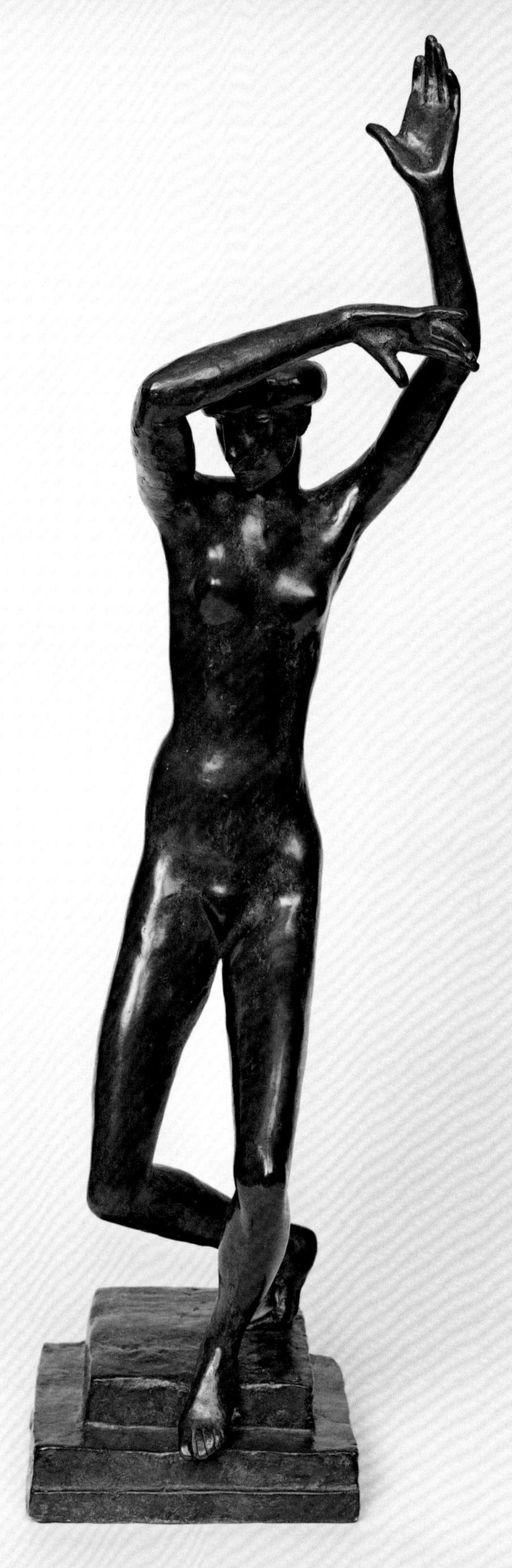

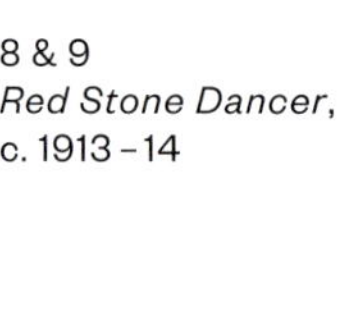

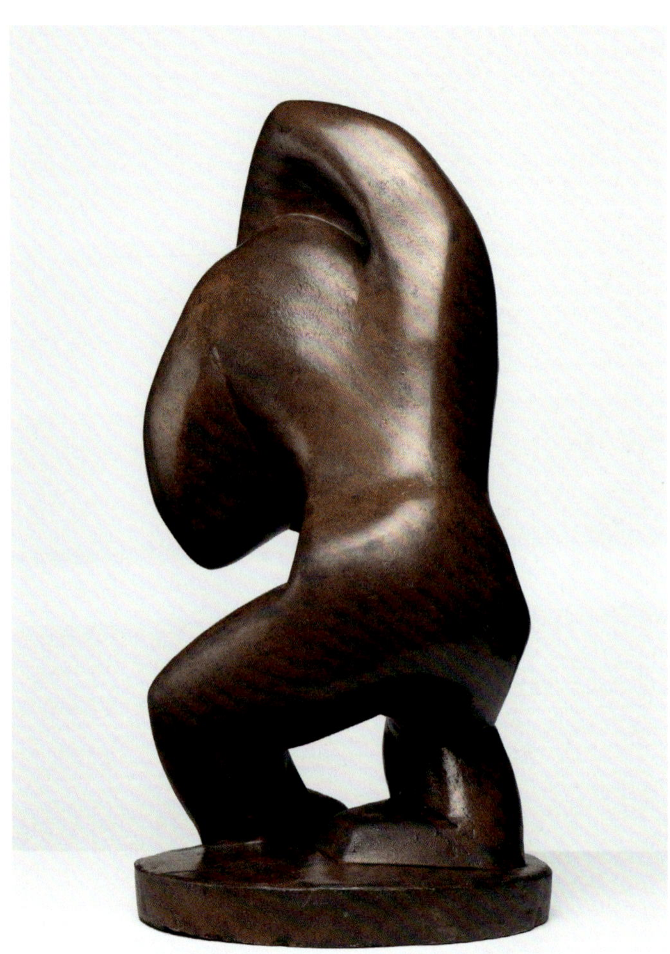

20

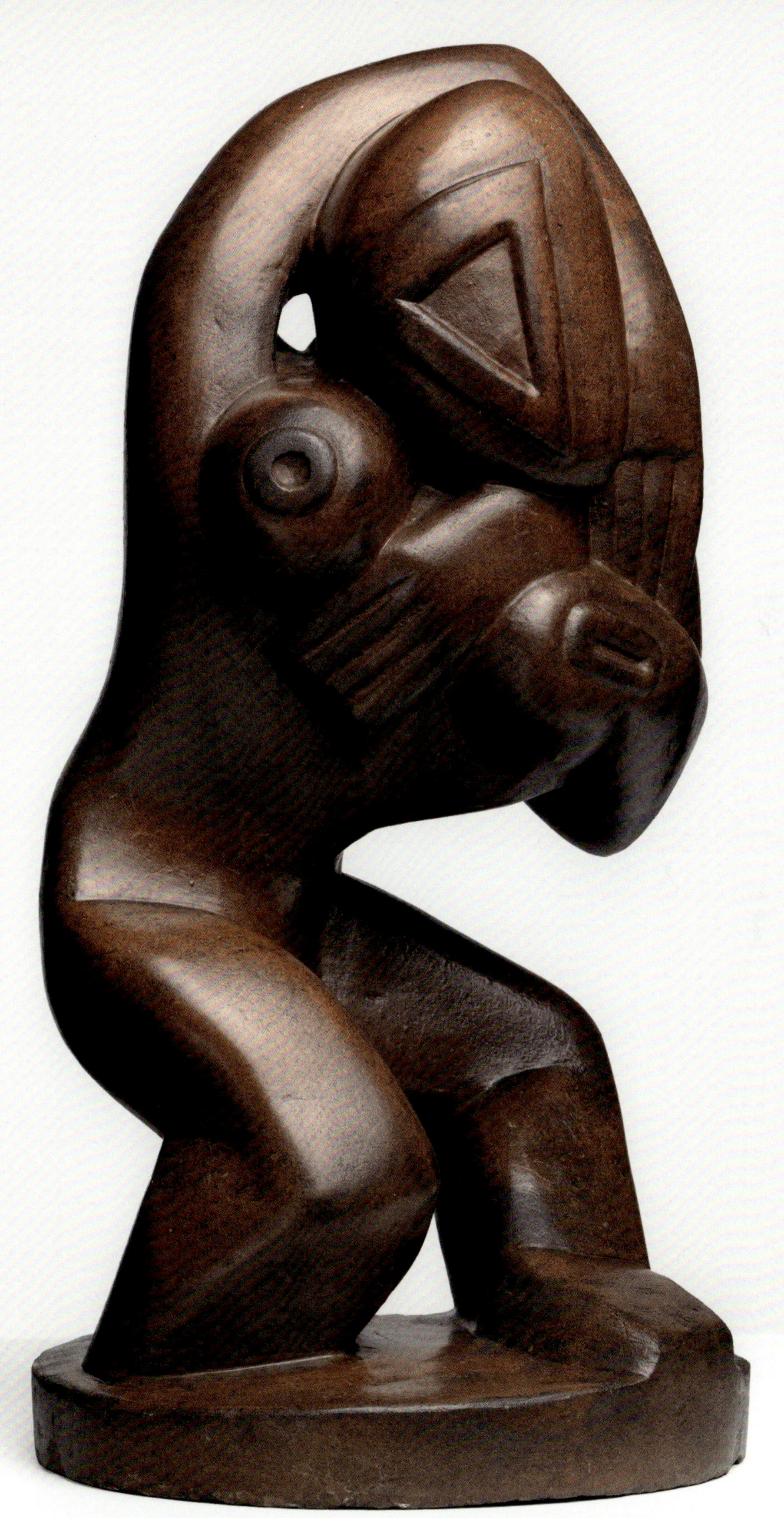

In search of NEW RHYTHMS

Jennifer Powell

'The great thing is:
That sculpture consists in placing planes according to a rhythm.

```
- - -      painting        - - - - - - - -     colours - - - -
- - -      literature      - - - - - -         stories  - - -
- - -      music           - - -               sounds  -
```

and that movement outside any one of these is not permitted,
that they are severely confined and limited, and that any
incursion of one into the domain of another is a fault in taste
and comprehension'.[1]

The French-born sculptor Henri Gaudier-Brzeska wrote this
passage to his Polish partner Sophie Brzeska in May 1911.[2] Even
the artist's arrangement of words and punctuation on the page
(fig. 5) are suggestive of 'rhythm', a quality that he prized highly
across the fields of sculpture, painting, literature and music.

New rhythms surrounded Gaudier as a young artist resident
in London between 1911 and 1914: they were, for example,
embodied in the vibrant colours of Gino Severini's Futurist
cabaret painting *The Dance of the Pan-Pan at the "Monico"* on
show at the Futurist exhibition of 1912, in the vital and
discordant sounds of Igor Stravinsky's musical scores for the
Ballets Russes, in the novels of D. H. Lawrence and the poetry
of Ezra Pound, Gaudier's friend and champion. The magazine
Rhythm was launched by John Middleton Murry in the summer
of 1911 for 'all those who support modern art'.[3] Murry, and his
wife Katherine Mansfield, equated rhythm with 'the essential
movement of life' and with a quest for freedom in art.[4]

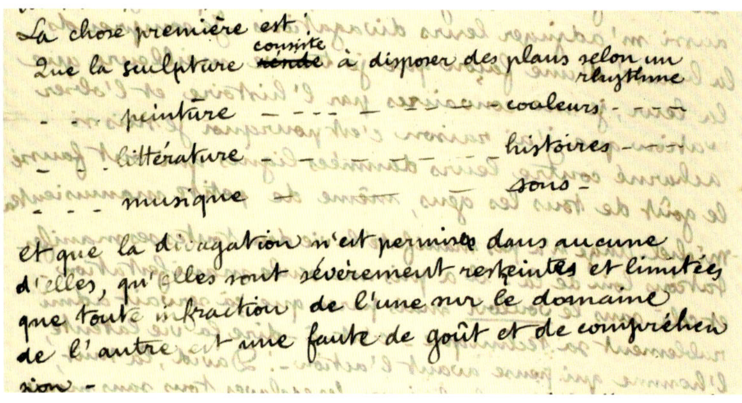

fig. 5
Letter from Henri Gaudier-Brzeska
to Sophie Brzeska, 27 May 1911, Albert
Sloman Library, University of Essex

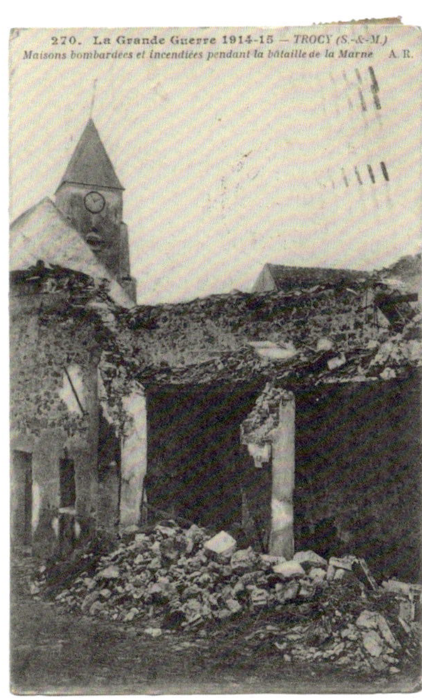

fig. 6
Postcard 'La Grande Guerre' from
Henri Gaudier-Brzeska to Edward
Wadsworth, 1 February 1915, AMC 5997,
Private Collection courtesy Archive of
Modern Conflict

Movement in life captivated Gaudier. He rarely reflected in any detail upon his sculptures or drawings in his letters to Sophie, and rather focused on the world around him, on the sources that he was quickly adopting (and sometimes as quickly rejecting), and on his relentless search for new subjects and new form. Some of the sources that informed Gaudier's sculptural vocabulary include the Renaissance sculpture of Michelangelo, African art from the British Museum and the work of Paris-based artists Auguste Rodin, Alexander Archipenko and Constantin Brancusi, and British sculptor Jacob Epstein; these artists were all experimenting with new ways to represent life through sculpture at the beginning of the twentieth-century.

Writing for *The Egoist* magazine in the summer of 1914, Richard Aldington described Gaudier as 'a wild unkempt barbarian';[5] Pound too recalled his first encounter with this 'bright-eyed wild thing' in his memoir of the artist (1916).[6] Gaudier's artistic output between 1911 and 1915, the period of this exhibition's focus, was prolific. In May 1910 he declared his intention to turn to sculpture.[7] Apart from early sketchbooks, the vast majority of the estimated 115 sculptures and 2000 drawings that he produced were made after his move, with Sophie, to London in January 1911.[8] Four years later, however, the colours, stories and sounds of the city were replaced by 'the bursting shells, the volleys, wire entanglements, motors, the chaos of battle'.[9] This 'wild' artist enlisted in the French army in September 1914 and was killed in action at Neuville-St-Vaast in June 1915 at the age of twenty-three. Even at war, however, Gaudier continued to make art; he sent letters and postcards (fig. 6), requested sketchbooks from his friends such as the artist Edward Wadsworth, and carved small sculptures from wood.[10] In an article for *The Egoist* of August 1915, critic and supporter of Gaudier's work John Cournos reported that one of these sculptures was 'a small dancer'.[11] While nothing more is known about this work to which Cournos refers, Gaudier did produce at least four 'dancers' in his lifetime.

A 'little dancer' statue, which Gaudier gave to Sophie before 1913, is sadly lost, or destroyed.[12] His three surviving sculptures *The Firebird* (1912, pls. 4, 5), *The Dancer* (1913, pls. 6, 7) and *Red Stone Dancer* (c. 1913–14, pls. 8, 9), were displayed together for the first time at the *Memorial Exhibition* organised by Ezra Pound in 1918.[13] The latter two solo dancers are arguably the best example of Gaudier's tendency towards rapid shifts between an observed expressive realism and a vital abstraction of the body; however, they share a paused moment of tension as their twisting and turning bodies promise to release energy and movement. *NEW RHYTHMS Henri-Gaudier Brzeska: Art,*

Dance and Movement in London 1911–15 takes this group of
sculptures as the starting point for an exhibition exploring the
breadth of the artist's interest in the movement of the body.
It asks how, and why, Gaudier and his contemporaries engaged
so frequently with dance, physical movement, and combat,
and investigates the impact of the ballet and new dance trends
upon these encounters.

'A Fairy Story, Charming and Terrifying'

Gaudier first engaged with the subject of dance at the direction
of his patron, the artist and collector Julian Lousada, who
commissioned him to make a sculpture (pls. 4, 5) inspired by
Serge Diaghilev's new Ballets Russes production *L'Oiseau de
feu* (The Firebird).[14] This vibrant ballet had premiered to
critical acclaim in Paris in 1910, complete with a fantastical bird
flying on wires.[15] Its narrative was borrowed from Russian folk
legend and it was described by London's *The Sketch* magazine as
'A Fairy Story, Charming and Terrifying' when it was performed
in Covent Garden in the summer of 1912.[16] The ballet
showcased choreography by Michel Fokine, a musical score
by the twenty-seven year old composer Igor Stravinsky,
colourful costumes by Léon Bakst (fig. 23), and stage set
designs by Alexander Golovine.[17] According to Huntley Carter
the writer for *New Age*, this company's new and distinct offering
to the London public was ballet 'as an organism, as an entire
work of art, not merely an evening's amusement.'[18] In his
memoirs the writer Osbert Sitwell noted: 'I was aware for the
first time I had been given the opportunity of seeing presented
upon the stage a work of art'.[19] 'The Firebird' was widely
reviewed in the press. The *Times* commented on the 'luminous
entrance' of the ballerina Tamara Karsavina, but was less taken
with Stravinsky's musical score.[20] The *Sunday Times* called
the performance 'quite unforgettable [...] the suggestion
of palpitating fear and violated purity with which she
(Mme Karsavina) shrank from the arms of her captor'.[21]

Gaudier preferred to sculpt 'single statues' standing or seated,
but Lousada directed him towards representing a *pas de deux*.[22]
It is not known whether Gaudier experienced the ballerina's
'palpitating fear' or the furious rhythms of Stravinsky's score,
though it seems likely. He confirms in his bound list of works
(Kettle's Yard Collection) that the two figures were 'portraits'
of the principle dancers Karsavina and Adolph Bolm. In *The
Firebird* (1912, pls. 4, 5), Gaudier transposes something of the
feel of Bakst's costumes for the ballet in his smoothly modelled
figures' headwear and Karsavina's strange feather-inspired
costume. Diaghilev did not allow any of his company's
performances to be filmed, but we know something of Fokine's

choreography from later productions. Fokine favoured more natural positions of the body over rigid classical lines. Gaudier's dancers adopt a pose from the ballet's first scene – the attempted capture of the firebird who tries, in vain, to repetitively flutter her arms (or wings) away from her captor.

Photographs of the ballet by leading society photographers Alexander Bassano and Emile Otto Hoppé appeared widely in the press, in magazines and on postcards. Bassano's images, in particular, are a likely source for Gaudier's group (fig. 7).[23] In Gaudier's sculpture, Bolm's weight shifts backwards as he holds his muse; the leaning arch of her foot *en point* emphasizes her pull away from him (pl. 5). Gaudier chooses the moment of greatest tension and action in the ballet's narrative, yet the bulk of the bronze grounds this bird's flight.

The Firebird was Gaudier's second theatrical commission. His first was a sculpture of the actress Maria Carmi (*Maria Carmi*, 1912, Kettle's Yard) in her role as the Madonna in Max Rheinhardt's play *The Miracle*, which he had seen a few months earlier at the Olympia Theatre. Although Gaudier was not entirely happy with the profit that he received for *The Firebird*,

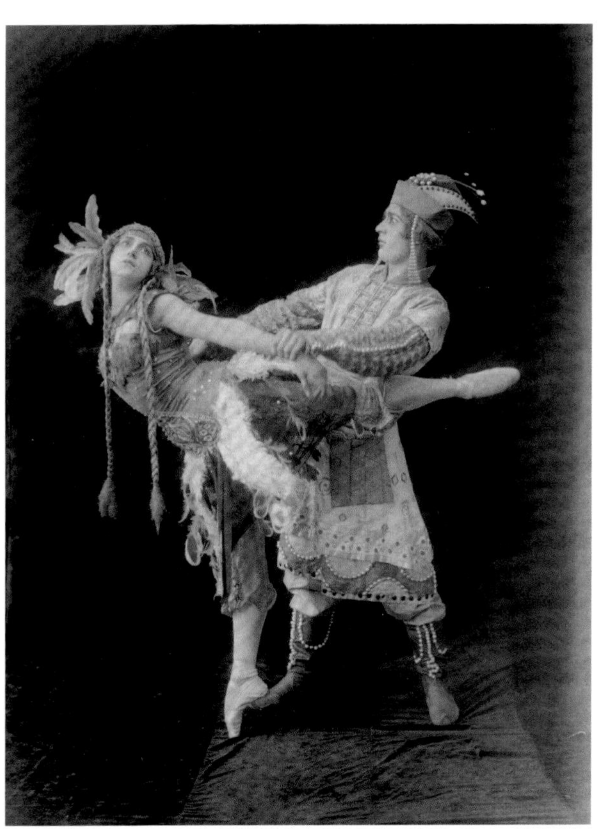

fig. 7
Tamara Karsavina as the Firebird
and Adolph Bolm as Ivan Tsarevich
in *L'Oiseau de Feu* (The Firebird) by
Bassano Ltd, 27 June 1912, whole-plate
glass negative, NPG × 81076, National
Portrait Gallery, London

these first two commissions were welcome for an impoverished
artist.[24] Encouraged by the commercial potential of subjects
from the stage, Gaudier tells Sophie that he will make further
small statues of the Ballets Russes which would 'sell well' when
the company returns, and of a work inspired by the company's
star choreographer and dancer Vasalav Nijinsky, whom Auguste
Rodin also modelled in 1912 (pl. 28).[25]

'A statue of a girl in a natural way'

In 1913 Gaudier exhibited a bronze cast (taken from the
original plaster) of *The Firebird* at the Allied Artists' exhibition.
It was his first public exhibition. The artist and model Nina
Hamnett attended the show and speaks of her admiration for
Gaudier's sculptures in *The Laughing Torso* (1932).[26] In this lively
autobiography, Hamnett describes her numerous sittings as a
model for Gaudier in his studio and the directly carved marble
torsos that he made of her such as *Torso* (1912, marble V&A,
resin cast pl. 10).[27] Hamnett's description of having 'turned
around slowly' for Gaudier during one of their drawing sessions,
may suggest that she was the model for his first sculpture of
a solo 'dancer'.

The Dancer (1913, pls. 6, 7), like *The Firebird*, was worked by
hand in clay and then cast in plaster and bronze. In contrast to
the Ballets Russes pair, this sculpture was not a commission.
The work is not recorded by Gaudier in his list of works,[28] but
its title seems to be taken from Pound's *Memorial Exhibition*
catalogue of 1918, where it was first displayed as a bronze cast.[29]
Hamnett was not a professional dancer, although she later
recalled dancing 'rather like Salome' at a Parisian cocktail party
with Diaghilev and Stravinsky.[30] In Gaudier's sculpture the
dancer's hands are sensitively shaped but her position, with an
outstretched arm and outward facing palm, does not recall a
pose from classical ballet.[31] Her naked elongated body descends
barefooted from her plinth. The *épaulement* of the torso begins
to turn the body, and her movement is emphasised through her
legs and feet stepping down from her base. Gaudier's use of the
figure's base to initiate movement in *The Dancer* can also be
found in *The Wrestler* (1912–13, fig. 22) where the figure's toes
curl around its platform threatening to dismount.

Art historian Serge Fauchereau suggests that Gaudier may have
seen, and borrowed formally from, a delicately modelled and
light-footed bronze Gallo-Roman dancer in the collection of the
Musée Archéologique, Orléans (near his childhood hometown)
(fig. 8).[32] As Evelyn Silber discusses in her essay for this book,
another likely source is Jacob Epstein's *Nan Seated* (1910–11,
pl. 20), which Gaudier admired on a visit to Epstein's studio.

10
Female torso, 1913

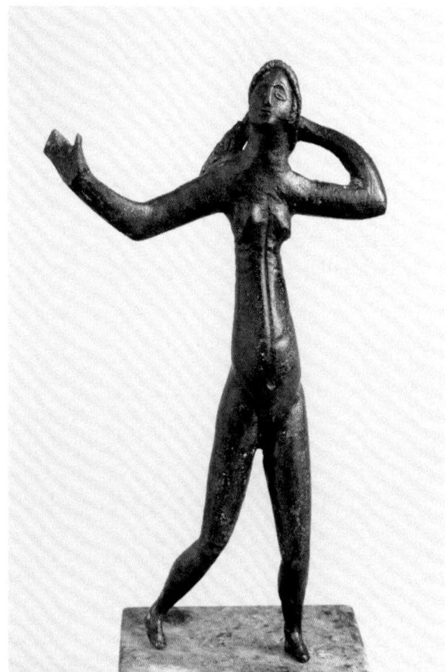

fig. 8
Unknown artist, *The great dancer
(La grande danseuse)*, Gallo-Roman
antiquity c. -100 – 99, copper alloy solid
cast, Musée Historique et Archéologique
de l'Orléanais, Orléans

26

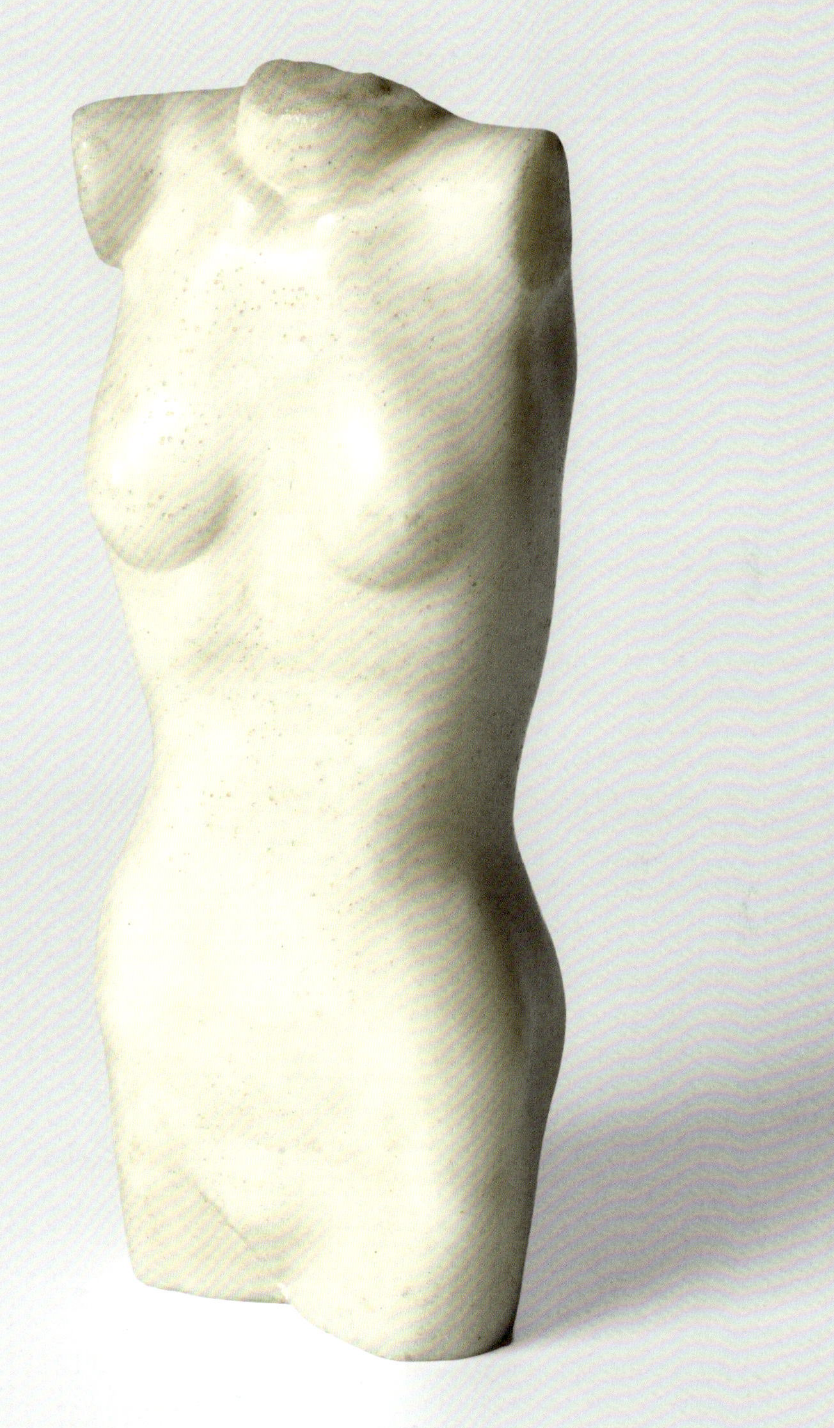

A further possible muse is Sophie Brzeska, which the creator
of Kettle's Yard, Jim Ede, supported in the first edition
of his memoir of the artist *A Life of Gaudier-Brzeska* (1930).[33]
Although there are some similarities between the elongated
nose and pointed chin of *The Dancer* and Gaudier's portraits of
Sophie, this work is primarily an exploration of the body in
motion: as Gaudier wrote to Smythies, it is 'a statue of a girl'
worked 'in a natural way to show my accomplishment as
a sculptor'.[34]

The art historian Stanley Casson poetically described
The Dancer in his book *Some Modern Sculptors* (1928) as 'a figure
in which movement is detected rather than seen, and detected
at a moment when it is neither static nor in motion [...]'.[35]
Casson equates the success of the figure's suggested motion
with Rodin's search for transitional movement, a subject that
is discussed at length in a book of interviews with Rodin
entitled *L'Art*, published by Paul Gsell in 1911.[36] Rodin insists
that 'movement is the transition from one attitude to another'.[37]
As Casson was no doubt aware, Gaudier read *L'Art* in one sitting
and particularly admired Rodin's walking figure *St John the
Baptist* (1879–80, Victoria and Albert Museum). Gaudier's
earlier admiration for the artist is announced in a drawing from
his Bristol sketchbook (1909, pl. 11) in which Rodin bows
before Gaudier's imaginary prize winning painting. In typical
chameleon-like fashion, however, only two weeks after writing
in admiration to Sophie about *L'Art*, Gaudier dismissed Rodin's
work as being 'limited'.[38] Gaudier's wider interest in studying
transitional positions of the body in movement is demonstrated
in four sheets of sketches that explore the progressive anatomical
actions of athletes running – one is annotated 'le mouvement'
(c. 1911, pl. 23).[39]

'A monster descended from the stars'

In contrast to *The Firebird* and *The Dancer*, *Red Stone Dancer*
(c. 1913–14, pls. 8, 9) was not modelled but carved directly
into a block of red-coloured Mansfield stone, from which its
name is borrowed. It is recorded by Gaudier as a 'dancer' and
was almost certainly begun in 1913 to be ready for exhibition
at the Alpine Club in January of the following year.[40] Although
the work did not sell in Gaudier's lifetime, he must have been
pleased with it, as he showed it again in March at the London
Group's first exhibition.[41]

At the earlier Allied Artists' exhibition of 1913, the British
sculptor Jacob Epstein (1880–1959) showed one of his directly
carved 'flenite figures' – fertile, totem-like forms, inspired by
African art (pl. 21).[42] Gaudier shared with his contemporary

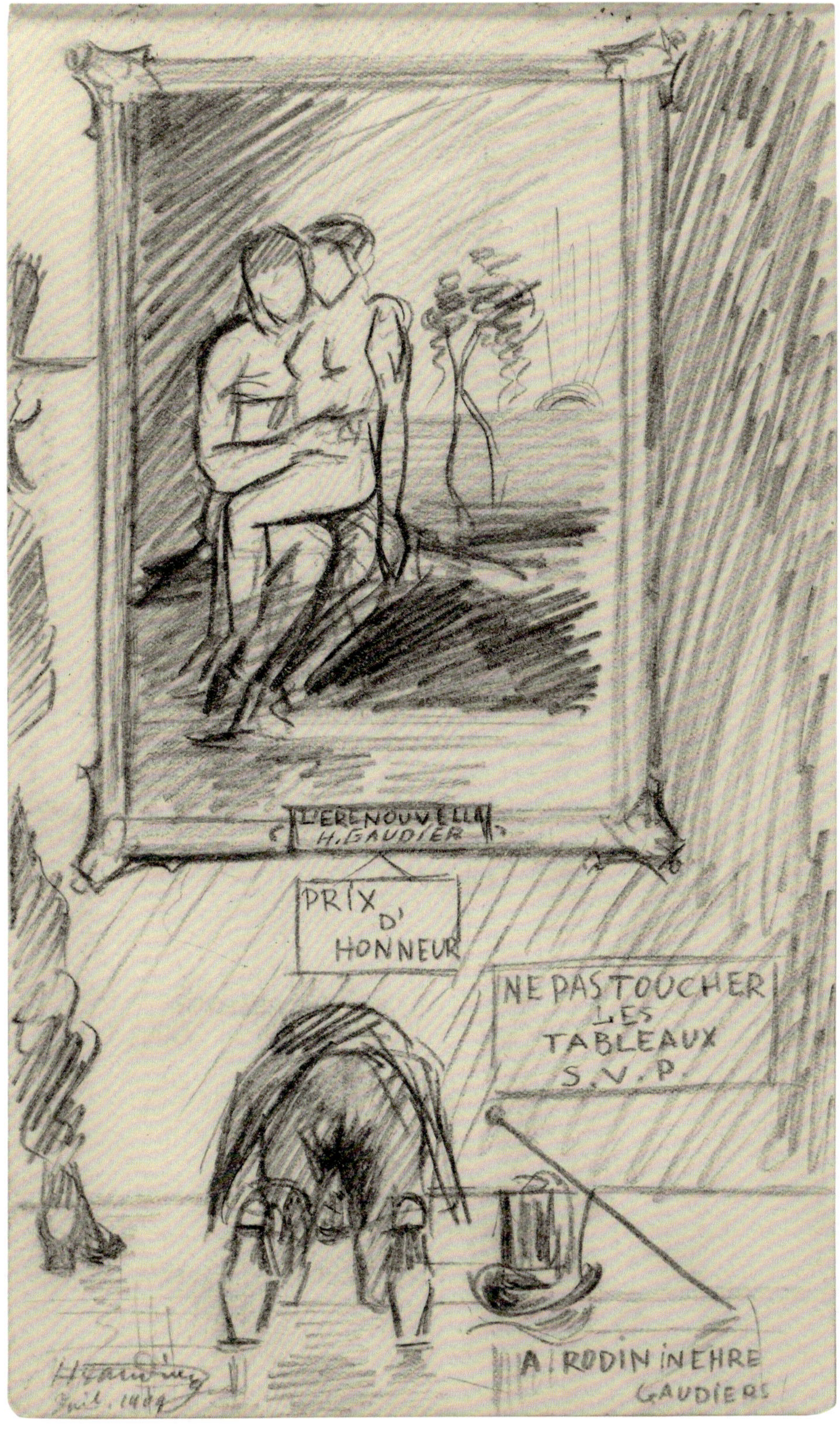
L'ERE NOUVELLE
H. GAUDIER
PRIX D' HONNEUR
NE PAS TOUCHER LES TABLEAUX S.V.P.
A RODIN IN EHRE
GAUDIERS

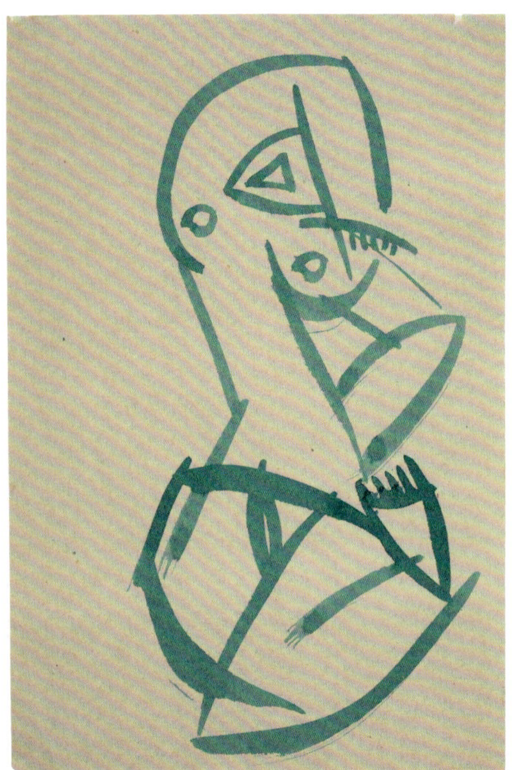

an interest in carving – indeed Epstein credited himself with Gaudier's adoption of the technique. The two artists also shared a fascination with African, Oceanic, Egyptian and world-art objects that could be studied at the British Museum. The Romanian-born sculptor Constantin Brancusi viewed this collection whilst visiting London from Paris on the occasion of the same exhibition. Brancusi was experimenting with the reduction of form towards abstraction in his heads, birds and fish in a variety of materials including highly polished metals. Polynesian sculpture inspired a series of the artist's recent heads that were shown at the exhibition, where he also met Gaudier. Sophie later commented on the connection between these two artists' works when she described *Red Stone Dancer* as 'a monster descended from the stars. Its resemblance to humans was very imperceptible. An egg head Brancusi style with a triangle for facial features'.[43]

Gaudier's use of a simple circle and triangle to denote the facial features and breasts of his naked dancer has been linked to a primitivist reduction of form to its essential elements, and to the artist's interest in the Chinese ideograph – a unique symbol, created by the juxtaposition of distinctive shapes.[44] In a sketch that Jim Ede gifted to the Museum of Fine Arts, Boston, whilst under the directorship of his friend Perry Rathbone (fig. 9), Gaudier animates these recognisable motifs with the movement of his brush and ink. Gaudier was inspired by Chinese and Japanese calligraphy, a practice that requires both physical gesture and movement of the body in its execution.

Jeremy Lewison has commented on the 'outright tribalism' of *Red Stone Dancer*.[45] In July 1914, Diaghilev's Ballets Russes returned to London, as Gaudier had hoped they would, with the controversial pagan ballet *Le Sacre du printemps* (The Rite of Spring). At its Parisian premiere this ballet had caused riots among its audience who were repelled by the rawness of Nijinsky's choreography, the ritualistic dances, and the relentless dissonant syncopation of Stravinsky's score.[46] Although the civil servant and patron Edward Marsh remembers visiting the ballet with Gaudier in the summer of 1914,[47] it is speculative to suggest that Gaudier saw *The Rite of Spring* in the previous year. However, the impossibly twisted stance and unnatural body position with inward facing feet of *Red Stone Dancer* resonates with the angular poses (and inward turned feet) of Nijinsky's dancers.[48] The bold energy of Gaudier's sculpture is further enhanced by the use of a red-coloured stone.

In three striking pen and ink drawings that are associated with *Red Stone Dancer*, Gaudier's focus turns to the possibilities of multiple dancing bodies or multiple movements.[49] Gaudier suggested that 'different parts of the body may move in opposed directions and with diverse speeds.'[50] The violent three-headed but double-bodied dancer, which was also published as an illustration in *New Age* magazine in 1913 (pl. 14, fig. 27), and a bending double-limbed dancer (fig. 11), embody Gaudier's description. Evelyn Silber suggests that the three-headed figure may have been inspired by the tribhanga posture of Indian dancers in the British Museum; it may also recall Hindu goddess Shiva who is sometimes represented as a triple-headed deity, or as the dancer Nataraja with multiple limbs. The snake-like, perhaps Salome-like, drawing of a double-figured temptress (fig. 10), brings a heightened eroticism to Gaudier's exploration of the dancer subject.[51]

Red Stone Dancer was displayed in the *First Vorticist Exhibition* at the Doré Galleries, London, which opened a month after the artist's death. In April of the previous year, the painter Percy Wyndham Lewis had launched his 'Rebel Art Centre' in protest against Roger Fry's Omega Workshops, and in response to (and later as a challenge to) French Cubism and Italian Futurism. Lewis persuaded Gaudier to align himself with the Rebels. In July 1914, the *Times* reported that Lewis' revolutionary art centre had developed into a 'Vorticist

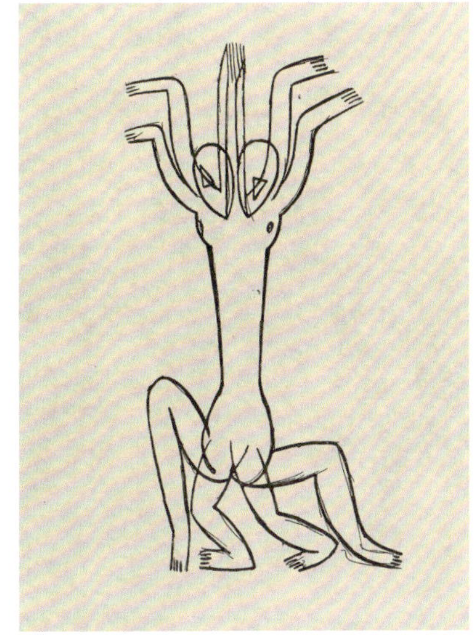

fig. 10
Henri Gaudier-Brzeska, *Dancer study*, c. 1913 – 14, reproduced in *20 drawings from the note-books of H. Gaudier-Brzeska*, Ovid Press, London, 1919, unpaged sheet, Cambridge University Library

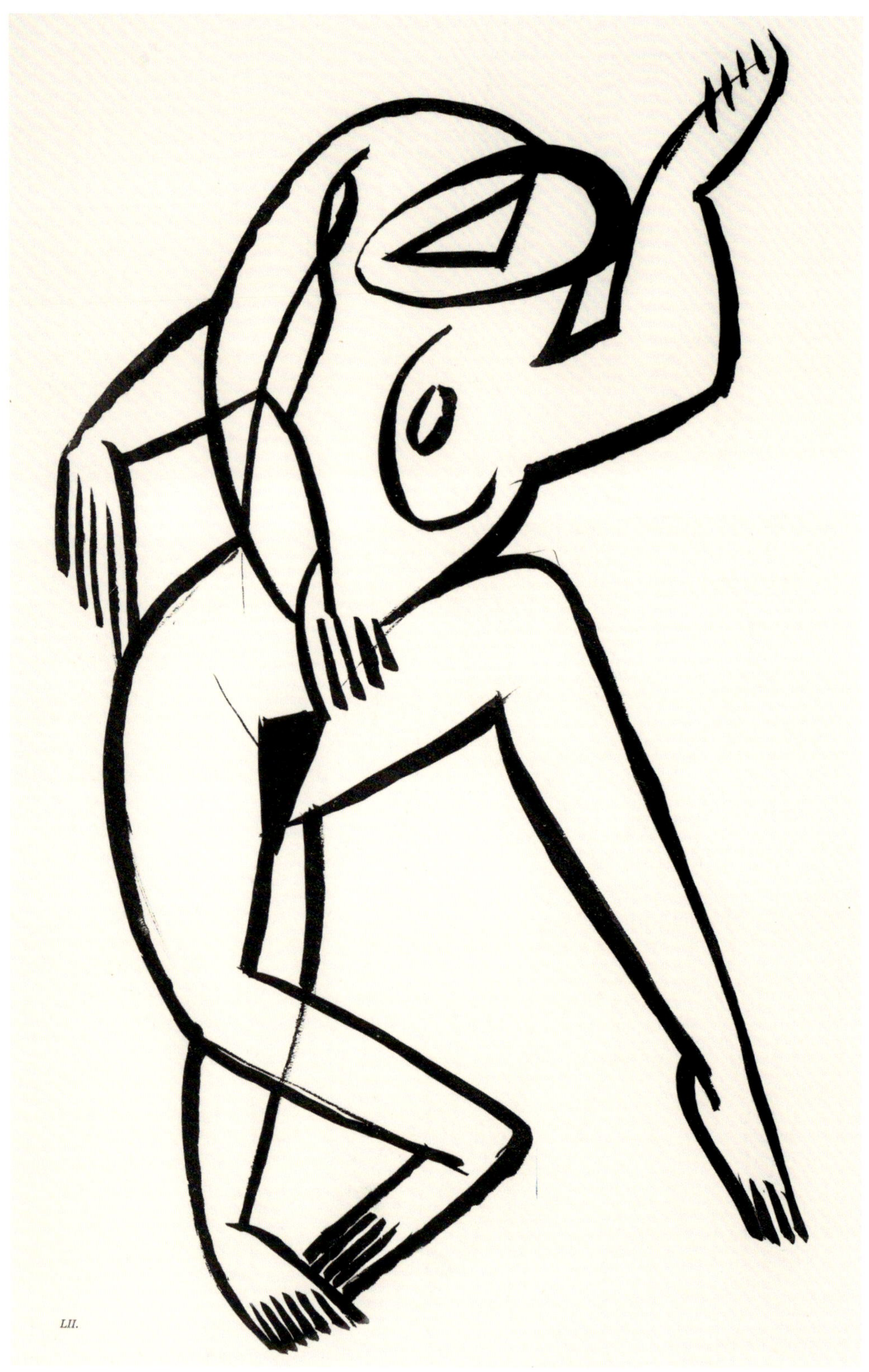

LII.

movement' and listed Gaudier among its members.[52] The article describes 'the vortex of present day life, the whirlpool into which the hustle and bustle of everyday movement converges'.[53] The twisting body of *Red Stone Dancer*, frozen in stone but waiting to release its energy from the block, embodies something of this 'whirlpool' of life, and the 'energy' of the vortex that Gaudier describes in his essay for the group's magazine *BLAST*.[54] In his two essays for *BLAST*, Gaudier repeated his proposition in the opening quotation to this essay, that sculpture should *only* consist of the placement of planes to define mass.[55] Two of the closest and most finished studies for the work (pls. 12,13) indeed experiment with the organisation of sculptural 'planes' on the page, delineated by graduated shading and crosshatched marks. The legs of *Red Stone Dancer*, particularly, show the stacking of angular sculptural planes, but Gaudier does not dispense with his figure altogether – viewed in the round, her body retains a curvature of form.

Drawing movement

As a child and young artist Gaudier sketched relentlessly on his trips to Bristol, Nuremberg and Paris.[56] He was proud of this work ethic, and of his desire to capture the world around him, boasting to Sophie in October 1912 that he had done 600 to 1000 drawings. Gaudier was stimulated by subjects that were in motion, or performing actions – subjects that were alive. This is demonstrated in the fluttering, futurist-inspired wings of his praying mantis (pl. 27) and in his drawings of a bird landing on water (pl. 26), a woman galloping on her horse (pl. 25) and a woman whose skirt is caught in a gust of wind (pl. 24). These studies from between 1912 and 1913 use a speed of line which, like his calligraphic ink studies, suggest that the artist is performing through the very process of drawing. Even in the life drawing studio, which he began to visit in November 1912, Gaudier longed for motion and for performance. He writes: 'I should have liked a model who didn't pose at all, but did everything he wanted to, walked, ran, danced, sat, etc.'.[57] A few days later he continues in further frustration: 'The people in the class are so stupid, they only do two or three drawings in two or three hours, and think me mad because I work without stopping – especially while the model is resting, because that is more interesting than the poses. I do from 150 to 200 drawings each time, and that intrigues them no end.'[58]

Modern dance and contemporary rhythms

'I obey no laws of the dancing schools and follow no precedents. I suppose, you know, that really I am not a dancer at all!'.[59] J. E. Crawford Flitch quoted the American-born dancer Loie Fuller,

who was famed for her swirling costumes and spiraling
movements, in the book *Modern Dancing and Dancers* (1912).
Fuller and Isadora Duncan challenged classical ballet
conventions and inspired modern sculptors. Doïna Lemny
explores this subject further in her essay for this book. Nina
Hamnett, the likely model for *The Dancer*, admired Duncan who
borrowed from ancient Greek poses.[60] Alongside this new
freedom of the body, dance crazes from Paris and America were
flooding London's music-halls and theatres. Dance was
popularised in the new short act 'revues', in cabaret clubs, on
film, and in public dance halls. As Lisa Tickner has explored in
her seminal book *Modern Life & Modern Subjects* (2000), the use
of the photograph transformed contemporary magazines in the
1910s. Popular magazines like *The Sketch* and *The Tatler* were
frequently populated with images and discussions of modern
dance. The former reported in 1913 that 'during recent years
ballet has suffered from the invasion of the one-act play and the
encroachments of the rag-time revue and has been temporarily
dethroned from its high place'.[61]

The new dance 'fad' was a quickly changing entity. 'Apache'
dance from Paris was the reviewers' pick from 1908 to 1909.
This violent duet inspired by the gang culture and sexualized
liaisons of the Parisian underworld, saw the woman flung across
the floor and violently swung around by the neck. It was
popularised in the 'Danse des Apaches' scene from *A Day in
Paris* at the Empire Theatre (fig. 12), and in French and American
films such as *L'Empreinte ou La Main Rouge* (1908) and *The
Mothering Heart* (1913).[62] A British production, *The Apache Dancer,*

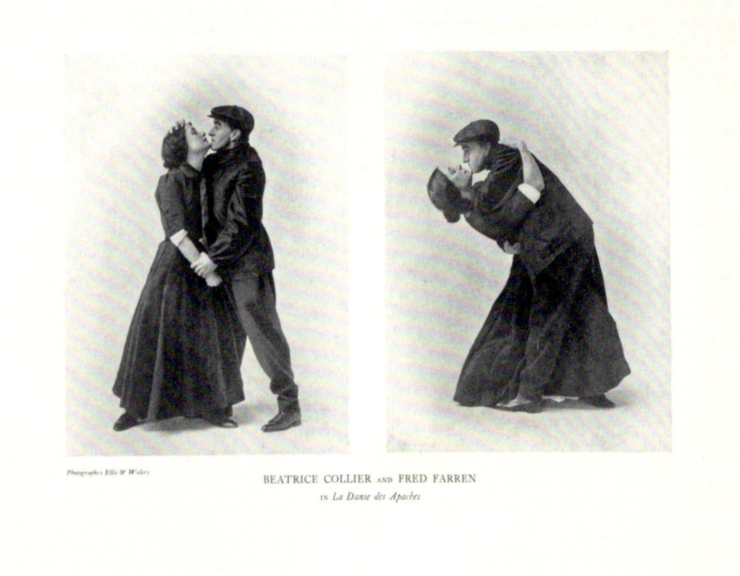

fig. 12
J. E. Crawford Flitch, 'Beatrice Collier
and Fred Farren In La Danse des Apaches',
Modern Dancing and Dancers, London, 1912,
plate unpaged

was also released in 1913. The Apache dance may be a source
for Gaudier's drawing *Man and Woman* (c. 1913–14, pl. 19), in
which the female's head is tugged back by her partner in
a position of sexual power and dominance. By 1912 'new
gyrations' from America had arrived in the form of the
Foxtrot, Bunny-Hop and Grizzly Bear,[63] and in 1913 there
was a Tango dance explosion. *Girl on Film* and *The Sunshine
Girl* brought this 'craze-dance of the moment' to the stage.[64]
The Ballets Russes' champion Léon Bakst (designer of
The Firebird costumes) made costumes for *Hullo Tango!* the
popular Christmas revue at the London Hippodrome in 1913,
and ballroom stars Maurice and Florence Lambert were
announced as 'the Nijinsky and Karsavina of the drawing
room' who were teaching 'all London to Tango'.[65]

Sophie recalls in her diary notes a comical drink-fuelled
occasion in Gaudier's studio where he began to dance 'the
'cake walk' – 'tango' etc. his eyes burning – his hair wild'.
'What was funny', she continues, 'wasn't so much the exotic
dances themselves – it was seeing Pik [Gaudier] the young
bear like nothing on earth with his great seven-league boots
jumping like an extraordinary buffoon'.[66] In October 1913,
Gaudier told Sophie that Epstein had been 'praising Strindberg's
Cabaret'.[67] This reference was to Mme Frieda Strindberg's new
London Cabaret Club, an underground dance club also known
as 'The Cave of the Golden Calf'. In his memoir, Pound recalls
that Gaudier 'came to the Cabaret one evening'.[68] This was
surely Strindberg's venue. The club brought together British
artists (including Spencer Gore, Lewis and Epstein) to decorate
its interiors and design its programmes, posters and other
ephemera. Helen Saunders' watercolour painting *Cabaret* (c.
1913–14, pl. 37) may also reference the club, which opened in
April 1912 and ran to February 1914. Now only known through
related studies, Lewis' remarkable nine foot painting *Kermesse*
hung on the stairs. In one of these studies, *The Dancers* (1914,
pl. 38), the angular interlocking figures push against the
triangular cage-like space that restrains their movements.
Strindberg's club offered Flamenco, Tarantella, Tango teas,
Turkey Trot and Bunny Hop. Sitwell later described it as 'a
super-heated Vorticist garden of gesticulating figures, dancing
and talking while the rhythm and primitive forms of ragtime
throbbed through the wide room.'[69] He continues 'dancing
more than conversation was the art which occupied the young
men of the time in the Cabaret Club.'[70]

The painter William Roberts engaged extensively with the
theme of dance. His pen and gouache study *The Toe Dancer*
(c. 1914, pl. 31), is a voyeuristic scene with an angular dancer
at its centre, set in the home of Stuart Gray. Gray offered artists

lodgings, life drawing classes (which Epstein attended) and threw wild parties. The Russian ballet dancer Maria Wajda, who visited his home, may be the subject of a series of dancer studies by artist David Bomberg (c. 1913–14, pls. 34, 35).[71] Like Bomberg, Roberts had resisted official membership of the Vorticist group, but the latter artist's works were illustrated in *BLAST* and he exhibited another dance-themed work with Gaudier's *Red Stone Dancer* at the Vorticist exhibition of 1915.[72] A pencil study (pl. 32), which uses Roberts' favoured grid method to work up the composition for transference to a larger canvas, and a pulsating coloured watercolour (pl. 33), are sketches for this lost painting. Richard Cork describes the watercolour as a 'resolutely modern ragtime orgy'.[73] In these works, and in Bomberg's dancers, rhythmic geometries and clashing colours are privileged over the figure.[74]

The rhetoric associated with London's dance trends was one of risk through close sexualized encounters, banned 'gyrations',[75] or new daring gymnastic athleticism. Training was advised for the Tango and *Girl on Film* was announced in *The Sketch* as 'The Dance Gymnastic', with four images of Dorma Leigh being flung around by her partner (fig. 13).[76] A number of calligraphic sketches of figures skipping, leaping, turning, jumping, and dancing (pls. 15–17), and a body of other drawings at the Yale Centre for British Art, demonstrate that Gaudier was interested in exploring gymnastic movement.[77] Rodin had also experimented with the physical limits of dancer's movements in his series of small sculptures entitled *Dance Movements* (c. 1911, pl. 30). These works, which were not cast or mounted on plinths by Rodin, could be rotated in the hand into bizarre positions.[78]

Dance / Wrestling

Alongside his dancers, Gaudier frequently explored combat in his works. He sketched sword fighters (1912, Kettle's Yard) and boxers in a poster design for the Black & White Whisky company (1911, pl. 42), in which the sinuous muscularity of the fighters' bodies bulge with brutality. Gaudier watched with excitement wrestlers 'whirling' and 'turning in the air' at the London Wrestling Club in the winter of 1912. His visits to the club inspired sketches, figures, and his carved plaster *Wrestlers relief* (c. 1913–14, pl. 49). Sarah Turner interrogates the subject of the wrestler in Gaudier's oeuvre in her essay for this publication. The artist's interest in the theme of combat, however, extends beyond the human subject to the animal world in *Bird Swallowing a Fish* (1914, pl. 52). Like *The Firebird*, the protagonists are poised in a moment of ultimate tension – the attempted capture. Cast in gun metal

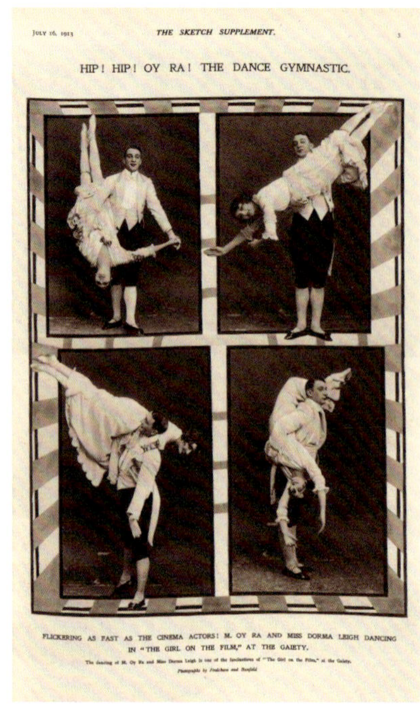

fig. 13
'Hip! Hip! Oy Ra! The Dance Gymnastic',
The Sketch, supplement 16 July 1913,
p. 3, Cambridge University Library

by Gaudier on the eve of war, this image of mechanized nature caught forever in an unresolved battle, has been described as a Vorticist masterpiece.[79]

Like dance, fighting was a popular subject amongst Gaudier's contemporaries and, as Turner discusses, images of boxers and wrestlers appeared frequently in the press.[80] Artists were also using a language of combat in their images of dancers. In a fascinating passage in Flitch's *Modern Dancing and Dancers* a spectator described a new American dance trend thus: 'the postures were those of wrestlers or swimmers, or runners or discus and javelin throwers, always proceeded by vigorous dance steps. And none of it was in the least feminine. It was dancing, but was essentially masculine from start to finish [...] there was more then a suggestion of strength and rhythm and of iron muscles under excellent control'.[81] Alexander Archipenko's *The Dance* (1912, p. 39) was reproduced on the front cover of *The Sketch* in 1913 (fig. 28). It is composed of two limbless figures locked tightly in hold: dancers perhaps, or is this a fight? In Helen Saunders' *Dance* (c. 1915, fig. 14),[82] two vibrant geometric figures flex their arms in a show of strength. Their position is comparable to Gaudier's sketch of a female figure who displays her muscular strength in her tensed arm (c. 1914, pl. 50). Gaudier was attracted to the athleticism of wrestlers' bodies, their large shoulders and necks 'like bulls'.[83] Seen from behind, the body

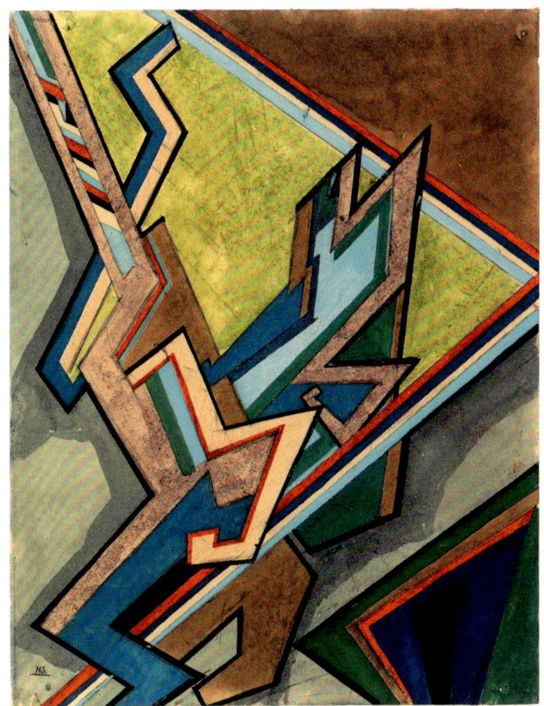

fig. 14
Helen Saunders, *Dance*, c. 1915,
graphite and gouache on paper,
375 × 295 mm, Smart Museum of Art,
The University of Chicago

of *Red Stone Dancer* is broad, even stocky and recalls something of Gaudier's earlier *Wrestler* (1912–13, fig. 22). His angular drawing of an imposing triangular female form with large legs (pl. 51) could be a sketch of a wrestler or for *Red Stone Dancer*. Given Gaudier's interest in athleticism and muscularity, one might expect his wrestlers to be violent aggressors. Yet a number of the artist's sketches on this subject, and his plaster relief carving, reflect more gentle and controlled encounters. One of Gaudier's designs for Roger Fry's Omega Workshops was for an inlaid wooden tray that is usually entitled *The Wrestlers* (1913, pl. 44). In both the preparatory sketch (pl. 43) and finished tray, however, the figures seem to skip or dance hand-in-hand. Gaudier's figures in *Wrestler relief* (c. 1913 – 14, pl. 49) share their elongated limbs with *The Dancer*. Their square hands and feet (with four, five and six fingers and toes) recall the feet of the figures in sketches for *Red Stone Dancer* (pl. 14). Their bodies are embroiled and tangled in a rhythmic pattern, but their pose is one of measured and choreographed grace.

Dancers fighting – fighters dancing, the visual language that Gaudier and his contemporaries employed was often interchangeable, but the rhythm of their bodies is omnipresent in these works. The greater liberty that dancers enjoyed in this period, their natural, athletic, or violent movements filled the magazines, the stage and the screen. It was from this mixing pot of new energy and freedom of the body that Gaudier's dancers emerged. With his three dancers we move from the stage, to the studio, and into the vortex – the ballerina to the life model, to the energized and subversive modern dancer. Common to Gaudier's dancers and wrestlers, and much of his drawing practice, is movement. As the artist writes: 'movement is the translation of life, and if art depicts life, movement should come into art, since we are only aware of life because it moves'.[84] But there was something more in Gaudier's frequent return to the figure of the dancer and figure (or animal) in combat. These subjects allowed Gaudier to experiment with tension of the body and form and with *potential* movement. In his review of *BLAST*, Richard Aldington suggested that 'he [Gaudier] thinks in form – in abstract form –instead of in things or ideas. He is perhaps the most promising artist we have'.[85] While not dispensing altogether with his subject, Gaudier pushed modern sculpture beyond the need for realism. He writes in *BLAST* that 'Sculptural energy is a mountain. Sculptural feeling is the appreciation of masses in relation. Sculptural ability is the defining of these masses by planes'.[86] Most clearly in his carvings *Red Stone Dancer* and *Bird Swallowing a Fish* Gaudier finds a tension, a compression of energy, that promises to explode into action from the sculptures' rhythmical planes. As Gaudier writes: 'Plastic soul is intensity of life bursting the plane'.[87]

1
Gaudier to Sophie, letter, May 1911, cited in Jim Ede, *Savage Messiah*, first published 1931. Original letter held by Albert Sloman Library, University of Essex. This citation and those that follow are from the latest edition of *Savage Messiah* publised by Henry Moore Instiute, Leeds, and Kettle's Yard, Cambridge, 2011, p. 69.

2
Gaudier adopted Sophie Brzeska's surname after their move to London in 1911. For ease of prose only, the artist is referred to as Gaudier throughout this publication. See Jon Wood's essay *'CELA S'APPELLE TOUR SIMPLEMENT JAERSH-KA'* for a the significance the artist's adoption of Brzeska, in *'WE the moderns' Gaudier-Brzeska and the Birth of Modern Sculpture*, Kettle's Yard, Cambridge, 2007, pp. 65 – 74.

3
Gaudier contributed drawings to *Rhythm* magazine in September and October 1912.

4
John Middleton Murry and Katherine Mansfield, 'The meaning of Rhythm', in *Rhythm*, London, vol. 2, no. 5, June 1912, pp. 19 – 20. The writer's supported the French Fauve painters' use of colour over the machine-age modernity of Italian Futurism.

5
Richard Aldington, 'BLAST', *The Egoist*, London, vol. 1, no. 15, July 1914, p. 273.

6
Ezra Pound, *Gaudier-Brzeska. A Memoir*, London and New York, 1916, p. 45.

7
Letter from Gaudier to Dr. B. Uhlemayer, 24 May, 1910, cited Ede, 2011, p. 26.

8
This number of drawings is given by Roger Cole in *Henri Gaudier-Brzeska. A Sculptors Drawings*, The Leicester Galleries, London, 1995, unpaged forward. Douglas Goldring records 1630 drawings in *Henri Gaudier-Brzeska (1891 – 1915) Sculptures*, Scottish National Gallery of Modern Art, Edinburgh, Leeds, Cardiff, 1972, p. 2. Gaudier's sculptures are catalogued in Evelyn Silber's *Henri Gauider-Brzeska: Life and Art*, London, 1996.

9
Gaudier, 'Vortex. Gaudier-Brzeska (Written from the Trenches)', *BLAST war number*, London, July 1915, p. 33.

10
Pound cites various letters in his *Memoir*, 1916, pp. 59 – 83. See also letters from Gaudier to Edward Wadsworth, Archive of Modern Conflict, London.

11
John Cournos, 'Herni Gaudier-Brzeska', *The Egoist*, vol. 8, no. 2, 2 August 1915, p. 121.

12
Gaudier to Sophie, letter, 28 November 1912, cited in Ede, 2011, p. 155.

13
Ezra Pound, *A Memorial Exhibition of the Work of Henri Gaudier-Brzeska*, The Leicester Galleries, London, May – June, 1918.

14
The Ballets Russes was founded by Serge Diaghilev in 1909.

15
Jane Pritchard ed., *Diaghilev and the Golden Age of the Ballets Russes*, Victoria and Albert Museum, London, 2010, p. 55.

16
The ballet premiered on 18 June, 1912. See anon. 'The Bird of Divine Fire: "L'Oiseau de Feu"', *The Sketch*, London, 10 July 1912, p. 5.

17
Golovine also designed costumes for the ballet.

18
Huntley Carter, 'The Russian ballet in Paris and London', *New Age*, vol. 9, no. 9, 29 June 1911, p. 211.

19
Osbert Sitwell, on seeing *The Firebird* in 1912, in *Great Morning!*, Boston, 1947, p. 152.

20
Anon., 'The Russian Ballet', *Times*, 19 June 1912, p. 10.

21
See *Sunday Times*, 23 June, 1912, cited in Nesta Macdonald, *Diaghilev Observed by Critics in England and the United States 1911 – 1929*, London, 1975, p. 69.

22
Gaudier to Sophie, letter, Sunday May 1911, cited in Ede, 2011, p. 69.

23
See also Beagles' postcard in the collection of the Victoria and Albert Museum, London, 1910; also photographs in *The Sketch*, 10 July 1912, p. 5.

24
Gaudier to Sophie, letter, 14 October 1912, cited in Ede, 2011, p. 177.

25
Gaudier to Sophie, letters, 28 October and 5 November 1912, Albert Sloman Library, University of Essex.

26
Nina Hamnett, *The Laughing Torso*, London, 1932, p. 39.

27
Gaudier's 'list of works', 1914, Kettle's Yard Collection, confirms Hamnett as the model. There are 3 torsos that are related to these sittings. See Silber, 1996, cat. nos. 59, 60, 61, pp. 264 – 265.

28
This works was added to Gaudier's 'list of works', 1914, by Jim Ede.

29
I have been unable to find a record of the title 'dancer' used for this work in Gaudier's lifetime. Roger Cole, however, notes the

existence of unpublished letters of 1913 between Gaudier and
Sydney Schiff who bought a bronze cast of the work. See Cole,
Burning to Speak, Oxford, 1978, p. 33.

30
Hamnett, 1932, p. 229.

31
The figure's pose, with one arm wrapping round overhead,
is frequently employed by Gaudier and many of his European
contemporaries such as Alexander Archipenko. See Sebastiano
Barassi, *'WE the Moderns' : Gaudier-Brzeska and the Birth
of Modern Sculpture*, Kettle's Yard, Cambridge, 2007.

32
Serge Fauchereau, 'Gaudier-Brzeska: animalist artist', in Jeremy
Lewison, *Henri Gaudier-Brzeska, Sculptor, 1891–1915*, Kettle's
Yard, Cambridge, 1983, p. 9.

33
In Ede's first limited edition manuscript *A Life of Gaudier-Brzeska*,
Heinemann, 1930, a photograph of the sculpture is entitled
Statuette of Sophie Brzeska: The Dancer, plate 2, p. 7. Roger
Cole proposes that Horace Brodzky first suggested that Sophie
was the muse for the sculpture. See Cole, 1978, p. 81. Brodzky
does not make this connection in *Gaudier-Brzeska: A Memoir*,
London, 1933.

34
Ibid.

35
Ede cites Casson's passage in *Savage Messiah*, 2011, p. 190.

36
Paul Gsell, *L'Art*, Paris, 1911.

37
Rodin in Gsell, *L'Art*, translated 1912, London, p. 68.

38
Gaudier to Sophie, letters, 3 November 1912 (discusses reading
L'Art) and 16 November (dismisses Rodin), cited in Ede, 2011, p. 185.

39
Handwritten annotations on one of these drawing sheets
references the ancient Neried monument at the British Museum
(300 – 380 BC). Its friezes are populated with figures in battle
and action. Gaudier also notes the journal *Revue de l'art ancient
et moderne*, 'pp. 46'.

40
The sculpture is dated in Gaudier's 'list of works' as 1914.

41
Gaudier was elected as a founder member of the London Group.
See *Uproar! The First 50 Years of The London Group 1913 – 63*,
Ben Uri Gallery, London.

42
As Silber notes, it is unclear which of Epstein's 'flenite figures'
was exhibited.

43
Sophie in her *Diary*, fol. 129a, cited in Lewison, 1983, p. 47.

44
In 1913, Pound received notebooks containing translations of
Chinese poetry and discussion of the ideographic nature of the
Chinese written language after the death of Ernest Fenollosa,
a collector of Japanese and Chinese art. Pound discusses the
ideograph in *The Chinese Written Character as a Medium for
Poetry*, London, 1919.

45
Lewison, 1983, p. 47.

46
See Alexander Schouvaloff, *The Art of the Ballets Russes*,
New Haven and London, 1997, pp. 92 – 3, and Pritchard, 2010,
pp. 291 – 292.

47
Ballets that were performed during the season included *Le Coq
d'Or* and *Scherezade*. See S. L. Grigoriev, *The Diaghilev Ballet
1909 – 1929*, London, 1960, p. 110.

48
The Sketch described on Nijinsky's correography as a
'Twitching, Bobbing, Turn-Your-Toes-In, Cubist Dance',
in supplement, 23 July 1913, p. 5.

49
The artist's interest in multiple, simultaneous movements was
shared by Futurist artists such as Alberto Boccioni.

50
Gaudier to Sophie, letter, 28 November 1912, cited in Ede,
2011, p. 157.

51
This sketch was in the collection of Nina Hamnett when it
was published by Pound with the Ovid Press as one of twenty
drawings by Gaudier, London, 1919 (fig. 29).

52
Anon.,'"Vorticist" Art', *Times*, 13 June 1914, p. 5.

53
Ibid.

54
Gaudier, 'Vortex. Gaudier-Brzeska', *BLAST 1*, London,
June 1914, p. 156.

55
Ibid., p. 155 and 'Vortex. Written from the Trenches',
BLAST war number, July 1915, p. 34.

56
These sketchbooks are in Kettle's Yard Collection.

57
Gaudier to Sophie, letter, 14 November 1912, cited in Ede,
2011, pp. 144.

58
Ibid., letter, 17 November 1912, pp. 148 – 149.

59
J. E. Crawford Flitch, *Modern Dancing and Dancers*, London, 1912, p. 88.

60
These dancers' distinctive styles encouraged others, like Margaret Morris, to experiment with the moving body. Morris was the wife of John Duncan Ferguson, art editor of *Rhythm*.

61
The Sketch, 22 October, 1913, p. 90.

62
French film *Les Vampires* was also released in 1915. Tickner notes three further apache films advertised in the British trade paper between 1912 and 1913 in *Modern Life & Modern Subjects. British Art in the Early Twentieth Century*, Yale, New Haven and London, 2000, p. 256, note 39.

63
See 'Terpsichorean Terrors. Which are Threatening to Undermine the Decorum of Our Ballrooms', *The Tatler*, 27 March, 1912, cited in Tickner, 2000, p. 99.

64
See the front cover of *The Sketch*, 12 November 1913.

65
Ibid., supplement, 23 July 1913, pp. 6 – 7.

66
Sophie in 'Details for Matka' cited in Gillian Raffles, *'Matka' and other writings by Sophie Gaudier-Brzeska*, London, 2008, p. 32.

67
Gaudier to Sophie, letter, 8 October 1913, cited in Ede, 2011, p. 182.

68
Pound, 1916, p. 46.

69
Sitwell, 1947, p. 208, also cited by Cork in his extensive study of the club in *Art Beyond the Gallery In Early Twentieth Century England*, Yale, New Haven and London, 1985, p. 106.

70
Sitwell, 1947, p. 208.

71
Dancer Sophie Cohen, however, suggested that the artist's drawings were based on Bomberg sketching her dancing outdoors with Margaret Morris. See Richard Cork, *Vorticism and Abstract Art in the First Machine Age, vol. 2, Synthesis and Decline*, London, 1976, p. 392.

72
Roberts' lost painting *Dancer* is reproduced in *BLAST number 1*, London, June 1914, plate 8.

73
Ibid., p. 386.

74
John Rodker used one of Bomberg's dancer sketches as the front cover of his book of *Collected Poems*, London, 1914.

75
See 'Minus its Objectionable Features: The Turkey Trot', *The Sketch*, supplement, 14 February 1914, p. 3, which discussed the features of this dance that had been banned in New York.

76
'Hip! Hip! Oy Ra! The Dance Gymnastic', *The Sketch*, supplement, 16 July 1913, p. 3.

77
There are over thirty sheets of pen and ink drawings of 'dancing figures' in collection of the Yale Centre for British Art. Some relate to *Red Stone Dancer*, and others are calligraphic studies of dancers or figures moving. There remains doubt over the attribution of some of these sheets to Gaudier.

78
These sculptures may have been inspired by the Spanish dancer and acrobat Alda Moreno, or by memories of earlier encounters with athletic performers such as the Japanese actress and dancer Hanako.

79
Richard Cork, *Wild Thing: Epstein, Gaudier-Brzeska, Gill*, Royal Academy of Arts, London, 2010, p. 145.

80
For example, Roberts' *Combat* illustrated in the first issue of *BLAST* and Bomberg's *Ju-Jitsu* (1913, Tate) shown at the Whitechapel exhibition of 1914, in which Gaudier also participated. See 'To hold their own our boxers must learn in-fighting', *The Sketch*, 17 December 1913, p. 322, for a double-page article filled with photographs of boxing positions.

81
Flitch, 1912, p. 217.

82
This work was displayed at *Exhibition of the Vorticist at the Penguin*, Penguin Club, New York, January 1917, as 'Dance', cat. 67.

83
Gaudier to Sophie, letter, 5 December 1912, cited in Ede, 2011 p. 159.

84
Ibid., letter, 28 November 1912, p. 157.

85
Richard Aldington, 'BLAST', *The Egoist*, vol. 1, no. 14, 15 July, 1914, p. 273.

86
Gaudier, 'Vortex', 1914, p. 155.

87
Ibid., p. 156.

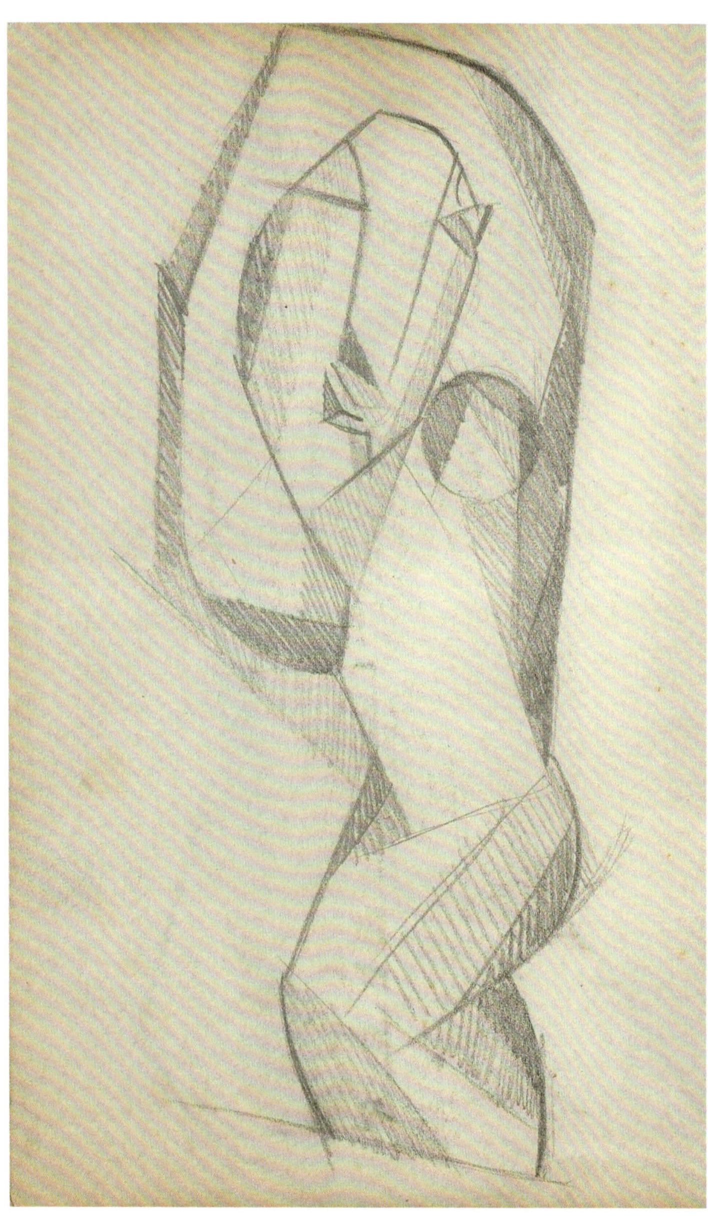

12
Page from a Chenil Blue Book,
Sketch for Red Stone Dancer,
c. 1913 – 14

13
Dancer on a yellow background, 1914

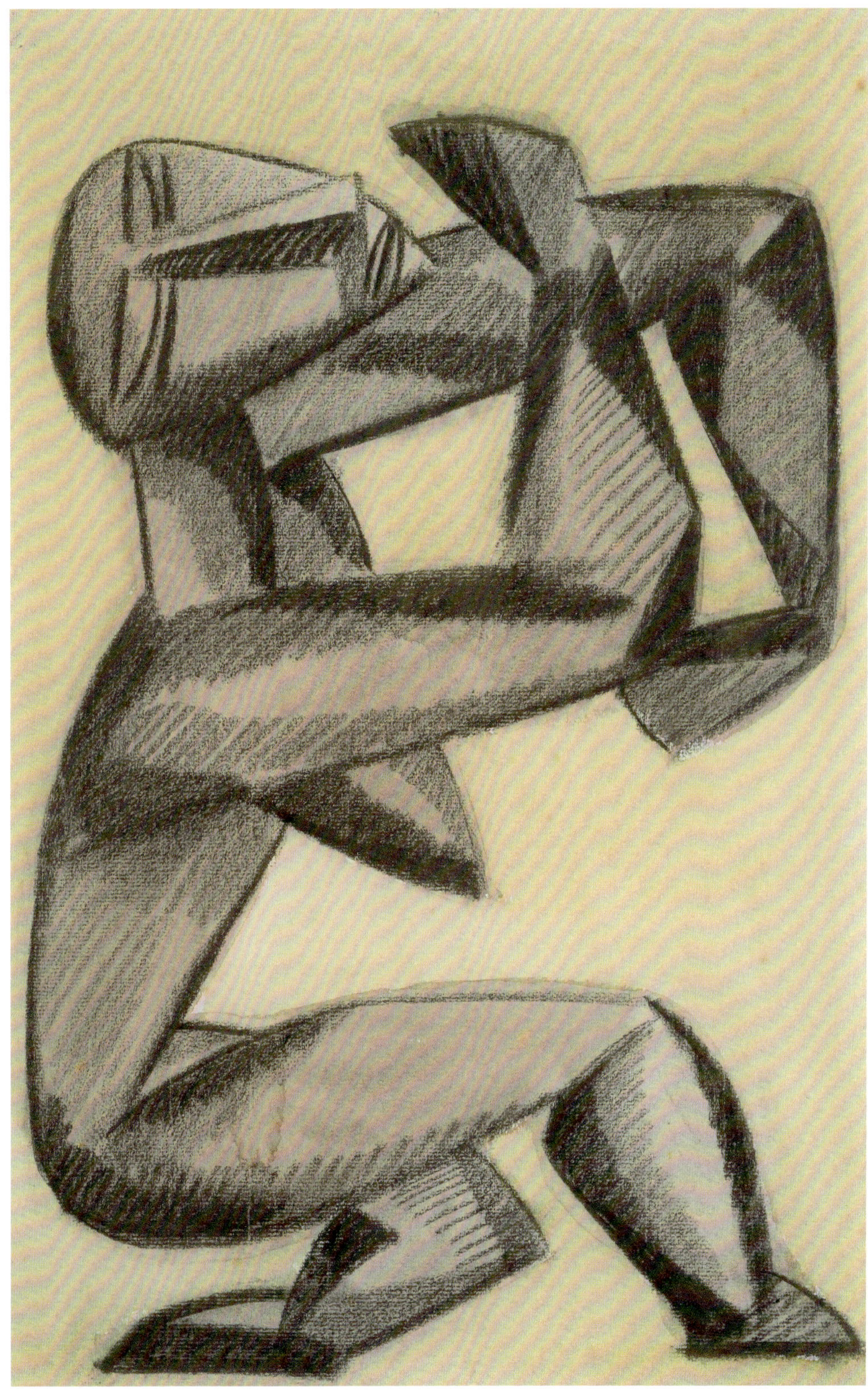

14
Dancer (study), 1914

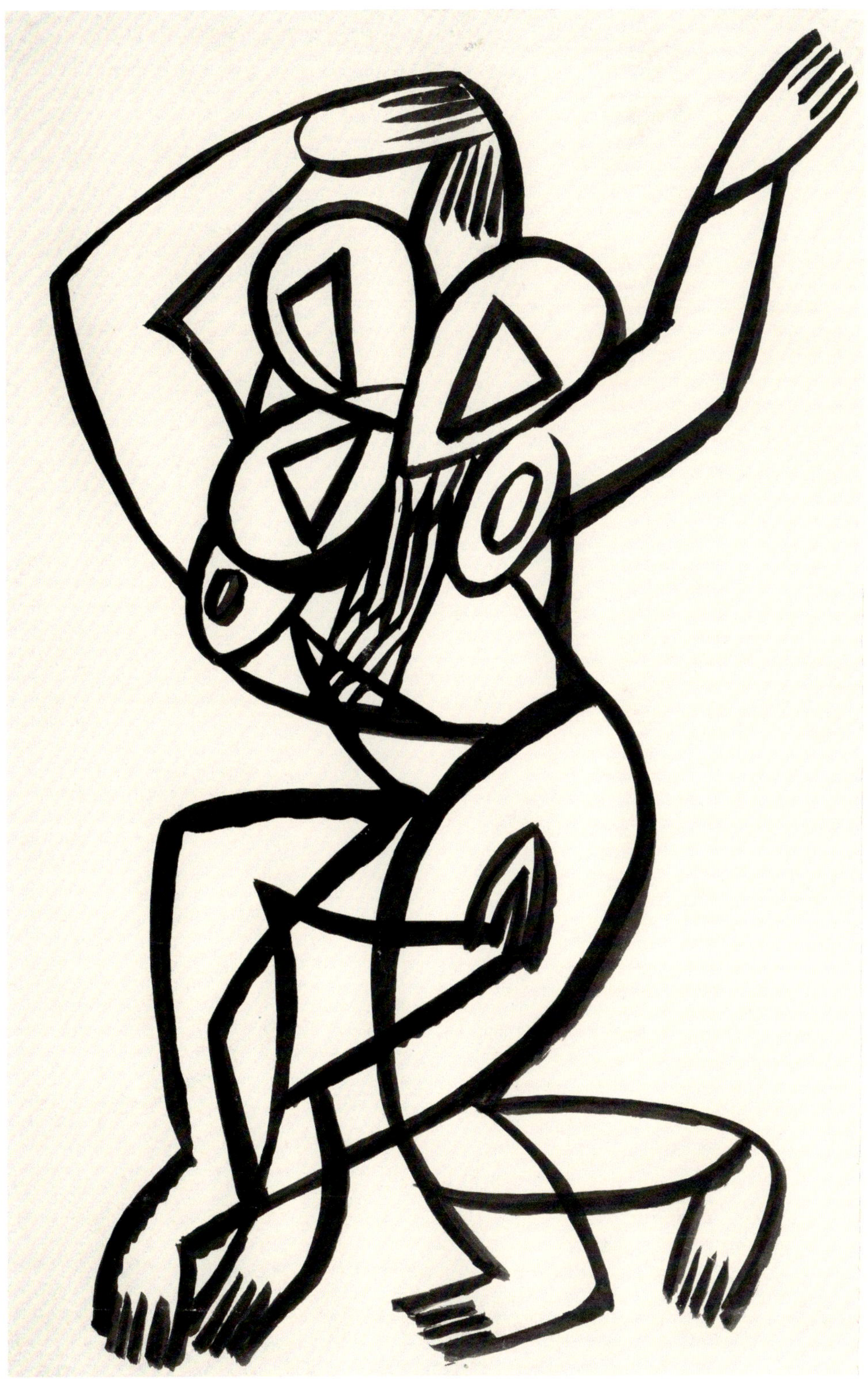

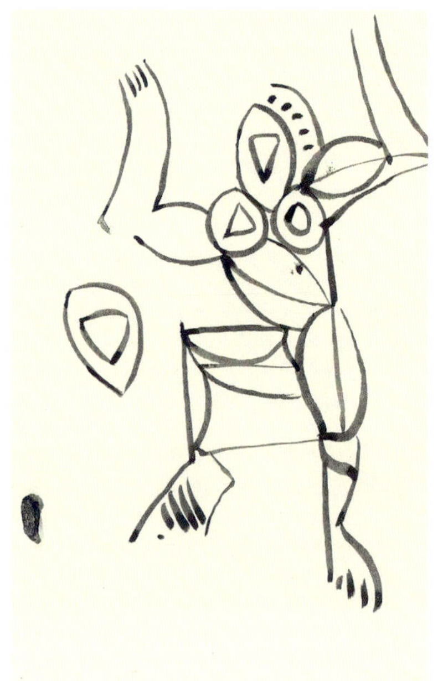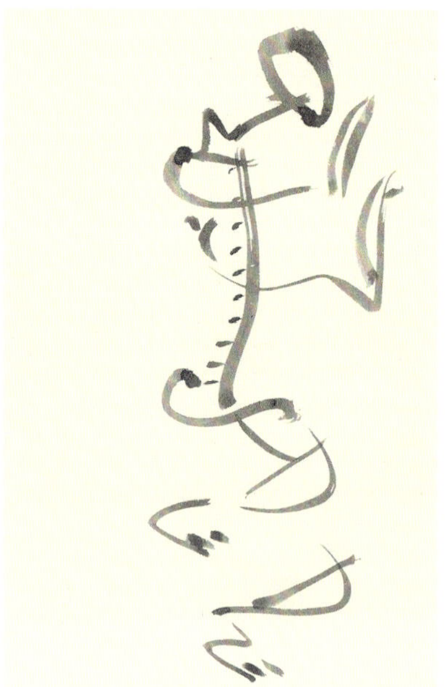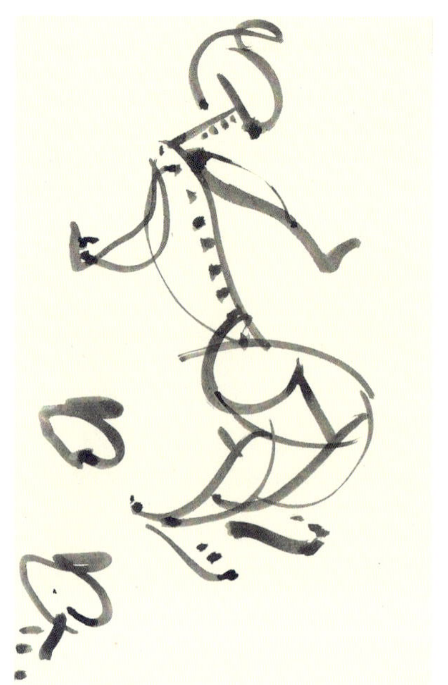

15, 16, & 17
*Three Studies for
Red Stone Dancer*, c. 1914

18
Female nude, c. 1914

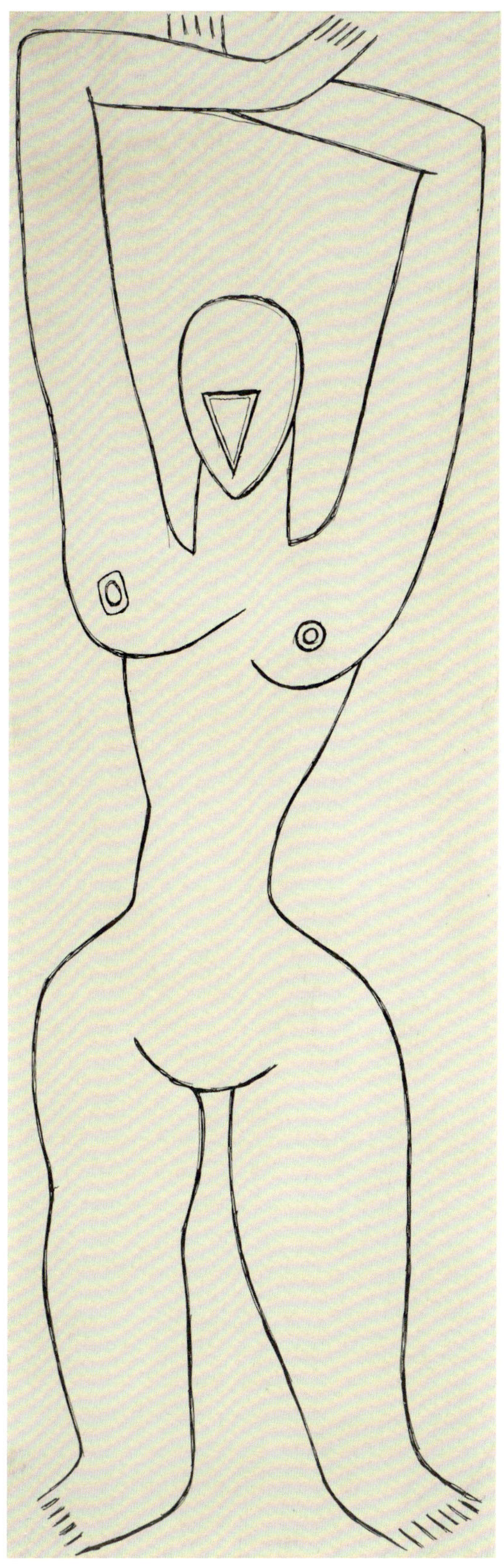

19
Man and woman,
c. 1913 – 14

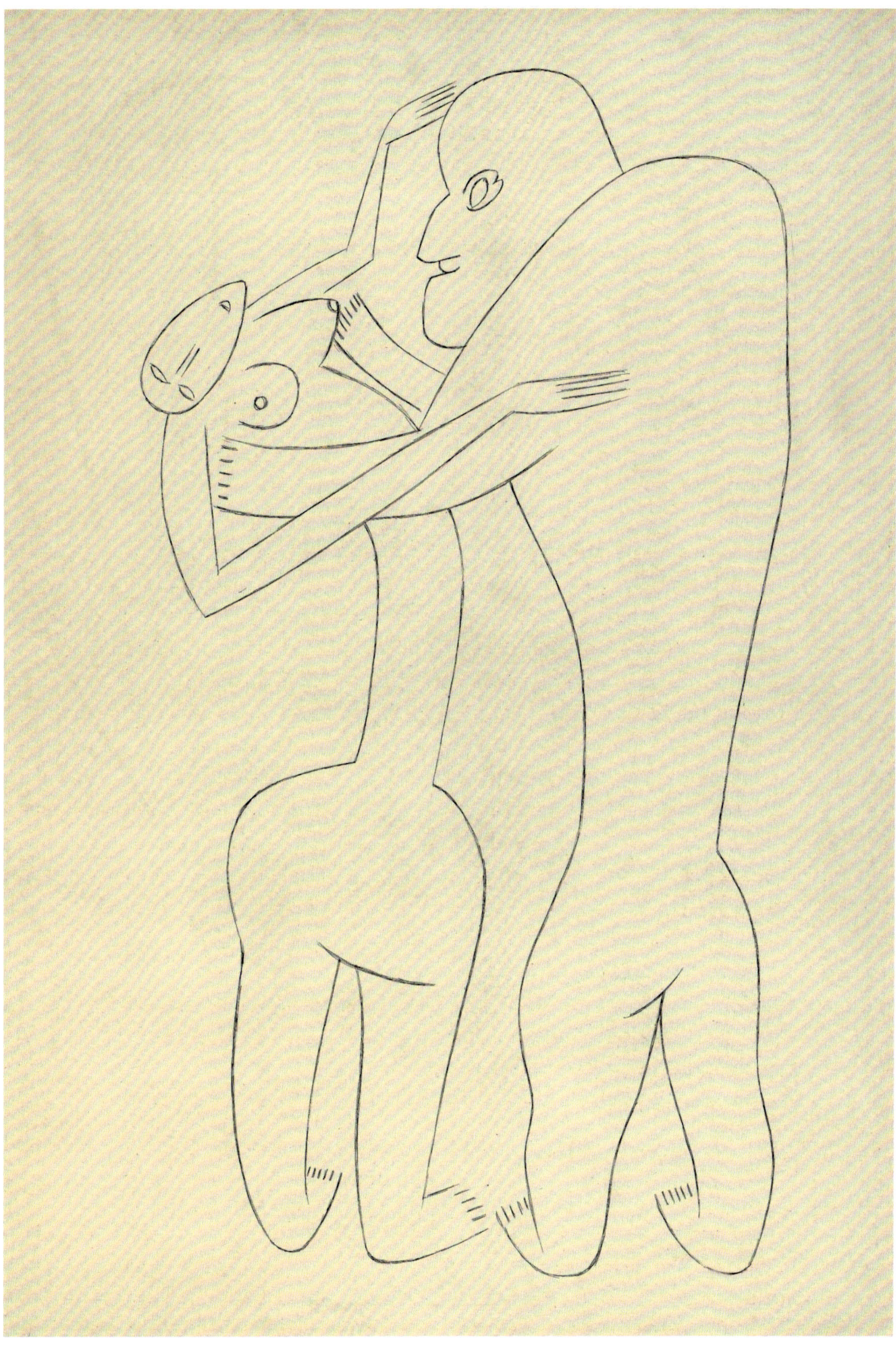

Gaudier-Brzeska and Jacob Epstein: Life and Life Force

Evelyn Silber

Henri Gaudier-Brzeska's relationship with Jacob Epstein was for the most part one of emulation. During 1913 and 1914 Gaudier was increasingly recognised as a vanguard artist in his own right – a rival to Epstein. The young Frenchman emerged during these two years as an articulate spokesperson for modern sculpture in his writings, and his work was seen to embody the abstract formal qualities and experimental vigour associated with the Rebel Art Centre and its successor, Vorticism.[1] Although the sustained inventiveness of Epstein's advanced work and his revolutionary mechanistic *Rock Drill* (1913 – 14) seemed to epitomise the dynamic Vorticist aesthetic, he stood silent and slightly aloof from this strident art-political movement in which Wyndham Lewis and Ezra Pound were the prime movers and which Gaudier embraced.

When Gaudier arrived in London in January 1911 the American-born Jacob Epstein (1880 – 1959) was already recognised as the leading progressive British sculptor. He had sprung to prominence through the controversy surrounding his first public commission, the eighteen over-life size figures, carved for the façade of Charles Holden's British Medical Association (BMA) head-quarters in the Strand, and completed in June 1908. Between 1911 and 1912 Epstein was widely known to be working on another large-scale, high-profile commission, the *Tomb of Oscar Wilde*, destined for Père Lachaise Cemetery in Paris. The completion of this huge piece of direct carving projecting from a massive Hoptonwood stone block, with its symbolic representation of Wilde as Sphinx, an Assyrian-inspired male nude in flight, seems to have brought about the first meeting between Gaudier and Epstein; it is recounted in mythologised form by Pound and more prosaically by Epstein.[2] The tomb carving was exhibited in Epstein's Cheyne Walk studio in June 1912 where Gaudier saw it. He enclosed a sketch and his impression of the piece in a letter to his erstwhile Nuremberg host and mentor, Dr Benedikt Uhlemayr, and while not uncritical, he was full of praise for Epstein's monumental figure 'flying slowly into space'. He continued 'the whole work is treated strongly – filled with insuperable movement and delicate feeling [...]'.[3]

Gaudier was already aware of Epstein's public BMA sculptures before the sculptors' first meeting. His small modelled mother

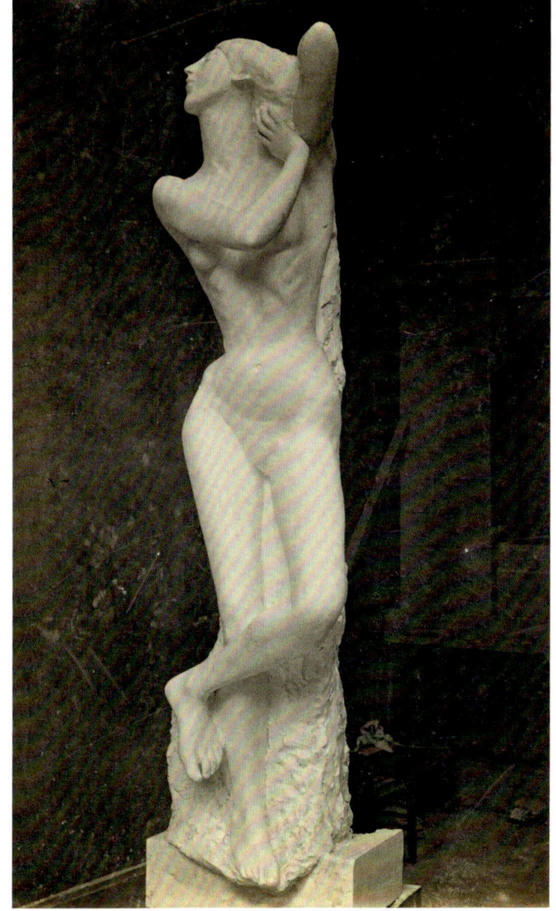

and child *La mendiante (Maternity)* (1912) is indebted to Epstein's *Maternity*, which was the most controversial of the BMA figures.[4] Gaudier would also have observed four male nudes and two females on the façade, stretching and twisting within the confines of their narrow embrasures.[5] Epstein described these carvings as representing 'youth, joy in life, youths and maidens reaching stretching arms towards each other […] figures, joyous, energetic and mystical.'[6]

Epstein's choice of words reflects his reading of Walt Whitman's poetry, a lifelong touchstone for the physicality and uninhibited sensual expression which was one of the most contentious aspects of his sculpture. The male BMA figures reveal his debts to Michelangelo, Rodin and classical sources, but the naturalistic female figure, *Maidenhood* (fig. 15), which appears twice, viewed from different angles, as the twelfth and thirteenth of the sequence, has been identified with Indian sculpture, in which the bodily rhythms and gestures of dance are central. The distinctive sinuous posture and expressive limbs of *Maidenhood* (and other figures considered for this commission), seem to draw on carvings of female musicians and dancers, whose triple bending, curvaceous *tribhanga* postures are derived from the swaying, sensuous movements of temple dancers.[7] A specific source may be an eleventh-century figure adorning a column base, probably from a Jain shrine in Gujerat, then prominently displayed in the British Museum.[8] There is no direct evidence that Gaudier especially registered Epstein's figure, but the multi-limbed, triple-headed study for *Red Stone Dancer* (*Dancer (study)*, 1914, pl. 14) may also reference Indian sculpture as well as the reiterated forms of Futurist painting.

A visit to Epstein's studio on 24 November 1912 provided direct inspiration which came to fruition some eighteen months later in *The Dancer* (1913, pls. 6, 7). As Gaudier recalled: 'He [Epstein] showed me a little bronze, very beautiful, quite the nicest work of his I have seen – alive and sincere – a seated woman with her arms above her head.'[9] In this piece, *Nan Seated* (1910–11, pl. 20), and its companion *Nan Reclining* (1911, Fitzwilliam Museum, University of Cambridge), Epstein explores 'a more intensive way of working' by making 'studies from the model, that were as exact as I could make them.'[10] In both works the movements of the model, Nan Condron are arrested, as if she is caught in some everyday activity such as putting up her hair. Judging from her long limbs and bony profile, Condron is likely to have been the life model for *Maidenhood*. The conception of the figure is conventional, unusual only in its naturalism, which contrasts with the still classically derived, idealised figures normative in the work of most contemporary sculptors. Gaudier's attention to Epstein's handling of the figure would have been sharpened by his own current work, since he had just completed studies of the dancers from the Ballets Russes, including *The Firebird* (1912, pls. 4, 5) and a plaster figure of Nijinsky (lost) as well as a group of two women running which, he suggested, could be an allegory of 'the Spirit of Liberty drawing women towards a nobler life'.[11]

A few days later, following a visit to the British Museum 'to the primitive statues – negro, yellow, red and the white races, Gothic and Greek', Gaudier reflected on his responses to primitive and European sculpture, focusing on their contrasting handling of movement and emotional expression. He concluded:

'Men do not move in one movement as with the primitives: the movement is composed, is an uninterrupted sequence of other movements themselves divisible and different parts of the body may move in opposed directions and with diverse speeds. Movement is the translation of life, and if art depicts life, movement should come into art, since we are only aware of life because it moves.'[12]

Movement in primitive sculpture – 'a large movement, synthesised and directed to one end' – he considered 'a fabrication of the mind' and 'a misconception of true movement'.[13] For all the swift changes of direction and thought that characterise his headlong artistic development, this passage has enduring significance in that Gaudier never entirely rejected the subtle expression of observed life in his work. The ambivalence of his sculptural output between naturalism and abstraction has been at the heart of subsequent critical debate about the direction the young artist's work might have taken had he survived the Great War.

fig. 16
Jacob Epstein, *Study for Flenite Figure,* c. 1913, crayon on paper, 686 × 425 mm, Private Collection, California

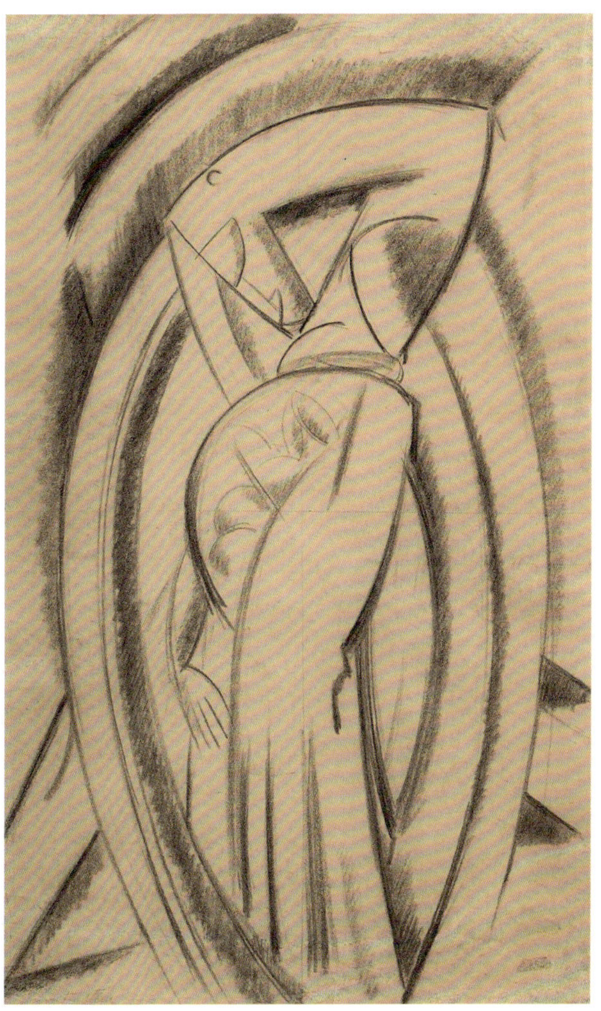

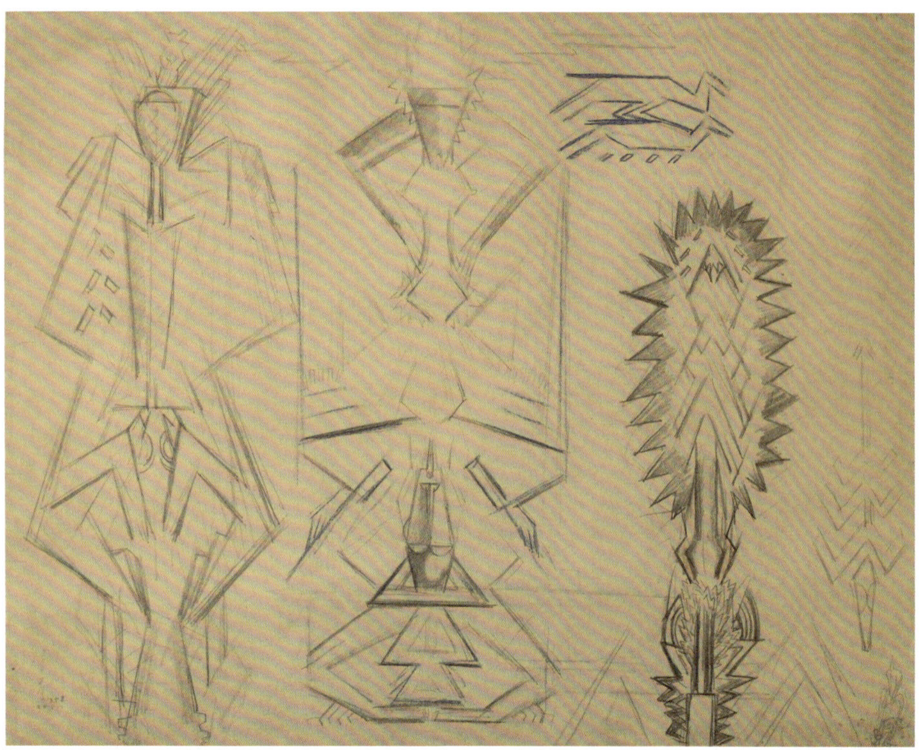

Gaudier's *The Dancer* (1913, pls. 6, 7) modelled on the painter Nina Hamnett during the summer or autumn of 1913, raises *Nan seated* to her feet; on the point of descending from the plinth, the figure moves from art to life. For the critic Stanley Casson, who considered it the artist's masterpiece, *The Dancer* was an embodiment of what Rodin meant by movement as 'transition': 'There is no representation of motion here, only its full and direct expression'.[14] The confident linear fluency of this dancer figure stems from Gaudier's rigorous self-taught draughtsmanship. His practice of sketching in the streets, libraries, cafes, parks and zoo, honed the economy and energy of his line, enabling him to capture human and animal movement in rapid, unhesitating strokes. His intuitive approach was reinforced by reading Henri Bergson's *Evolution Créatrice* (1907) and through his contacts with John Duncan Fergusson, Middleton Murry and others involved with the short-lived magazine *Rhythm*. *The Dancer* inhabits a Bergsonian world of creative energy, interactive rhythms and blurred temporal and spatial boundaries.

Comparisons between Epstein and Gaudier have typically focused on their outsider status, shared admiration for the sculpture of ancient and 'primitive' cultures, espousal of direct carving, and conception of carved sculpture as increasingly

fig. 17
Jacob Epstein, *Six Studies for Rock Drill, Venus and Doves*, c. 1913, pencil and crayon, 455 × 585 mm, Private Collection, California

abstract compositions of mass and form.[15] The creative emulation implicit in Gaudier's *Bird Swallowing a Fish* (1914, pl. 52) as a riposte to Epstein's series of mating *Doves*, or Gaudier's pocket-size brass *Torpedo Fish* (1914) and *Hieratic Head of Ezra Pound* (1914), as two responses to Epstein's *Rock Drill* (1913–14) are often cited examples.[16] Movement is perhaps the area where the differences between them during 1913 and 1914 become apparent – the abstract geometric dynamism of Epstein and the observation-based, living quality perceptible in even Gaudier's more 'abstract' pieces (*Bird Swallowing a Fish* being an outstanding example). They point to their very different preoccupations – the sexually driven, generative force common to mankind with Epstein and Gaudier's fundamental empathetic observation of nature that was never entirely eradicated by his increasingly abstract conception of sculpture as mass and plane.[17]

Epstein's carved figures are nearly always four-square, symmetrical, confronting the viewer, and carry an air of permanence and hieratic monumentality whatever their scale. The smaller flenite pieces were described by Hulme, who first owned *Female Figure in Flenite* (1913, pl. 21), as having 'a certain quality of inevitableness about them which makes them seem like things discovered rather than things constituted.'[18] Yet they do not lack energy; the smooth, compressed masses and shallow relief-like incisions of Epstein's two flenite figures (the other being *Figure in Flenite* (1913–14, Minneapolis Institute of Arts) and *Flenite Relief* (1913–14, Leeds City Art Gallery), recently identified by Jon Wood as condensing into its shallow depth the arched body of a woman giving birth, create almost a force field around them.[19] That explosive, generative energy is visible in the reiterated curves and zigzags that surround the contemplative pregnant female at the centre of *Study for Figure in Flenite* (fig. 16), in the zigzags and diagonals that create the abstract geometric dynamism of the hair/sunrays/petals of *Sunflower* (1912–13, National Gallery of Victoria, Melbourne), and in the *Six Studies for 'Rock Drill', 'Venus' and 'Doves'* (1913, fig. 17).[20] The conceptualised simplified movement of sculpture from 'primitive' cultures, against which Gaudier had railed, was readily transmuted by Epstein, with his profound admiration for these artefacts, into the abstract dynamism and aggression of Vorticism.[21]

Only in his small totemic pieces, such as *Doorknocker* (1914, Kettle's Yard) and *Torpedo Fish* do Gaudier's pieces have a comparably symbolic function. Asymmetry and movement, latent or active, are more characteristic, whether schooled, as in the costumed poise of the commissioned *The Firebird* (pls. 4, 5); hovering between violence and desire in the 'apache' dance drawing known as *Man and Woman* (1913–14, pl. 19); or responding instinctively to some elemental pulse in *Red Stone Dancer* (c. 1913 – 14, pls. 8, 9). The latter, 'an abstract sculpture in red stone', was exhibited three times between 1914 and 1915; at the London Group exhibition in March it was shown in the same room as one of Epstein's mating *Doves*, the lost *Bird Pluming Itself* and a *Carving in Flenite*.[22] *Red Stone Dancer*, seen then and since as a key work in Gaudier's growing artistic autonomy, embodies a vigorous torsion and primitivist vigour that mark the artist's growing commitment to the Rebel Art Centre and his determination to assert his place as a modernist sculptor rivalling Epstein.

1

Writings for *The Egoist* and *BLAST*, reproduced in Ezra Pound, *Gaudier-Brzeska A Memoir*, 1916, edition Hessle, Yorkshire, 1960, pp. 20 – 38.

2

Ibid., p. 76; Jacob Epstein, *Let There Be Sculpture*, London, 1940, p. 44.

3

Gaudier to Dr B. Uhlemayr, the letter's current whereabouts is unknown. It is partially reproduced in Roger Cole, *Burning to Speak, the life and art of Henri Gaudier-Brzeska*, Oxford, 1979, p. 22.

4

Evelyn Silber, *Gaudier-Brzeska; Life and Art*, London, 1996, no. 16, p. 254.

5

Richard Cork, *Art Beyond the Gallery*, London and New Haven, 1985, chapter 1.

6

Jacob Epstein, 'The Artist's Description of His Work', *British Medical Journal*, 7 December 1907, cited by Cork, 1985, pp. 35 – 6.

7

Rupert R. Arrowsmith, *Modernism and the Museum; Asian, African and Pacific Art and the London Avant-Garde*, Oxford University Press, 2011, pp. 24 – 56. I have identified an almost identically posed ceramic caryatid figure by the Austrian sculptor, Richard Luksch, which was reproduced in the readily accessible *Studio Magazine*, as a likely source, but both may have drawn on Indian prototypes. See *The Studio*, vol. 37, 1906, p. 166.

8

Ibid., p. 41, fig. 12; Rupert R. Arrowsmith, 'Jacob Epstein – the Indian Connection', *Burlington Magazine*, CL, 2008, pp. 742 – 48, fig. 34.

9

H. S. Ede, *Savage Messiah*, Cambridge and Leeds, 2011, p. 153, reproduced in translation Gaudier's letter to Sophie Brzeska, 25 November 1912, Albert Sloman Library, University of Essex, http://libwww.essex.ac.uk/Archives/gaudierbrzeska.htm.

10

Epstein, 1940, p. 56.

11

Gaudier to Sophie, letters, 28 October 1912 and 5 November 1912, Albert Sloman Library, University of Essex, http://libwww.essex.ac.uk/Archives/gaudierbrzeska.htm. Ede, 2011, pp. 127 – 128, 132, 312, 138 refers to 'plaster groups of Russian dancers' and to 'the Nijinsky'. The women running is on the modelling stand in the drawing reproduced in Ede, 2011, p. 132.

12

Gaudier to Sophie, letter, 28 November 1912, Essex University Library http://libwww.essex.ac.uk/Archives/gaudierbrzeska.htm; Ede, 2011, pp. 157– 8.

13

Ibid.

14

Stanley Casson, *Some Modern Sculptors*, Oxford, 1928, p. 98.

15

See, for instance, Dennis Farr, *English Art 1870 – 1940*, Oxford, 1984, p. 218; Richard Humphries, 'Demon Pantechnicon Driver: Pound in the London Vortex 1908 – 20, in *Pound's Artists*, Tate Gallery, London, 1985, pp. 54 – 56; S. K. Tillyard, *The Impact of Modernism: the Visual Arts in Edwardian England*, Routledge, London, 1988, pp. 155 – 6; Evelyn Silber, *Gaudier-Brzeska. Life and Art*, London, 1996, pp. 124 – 27; Penelope Curtis, *Sculpture 1900 – 45*, Oxford, 1999, pp. 84 – 5.

16

For Gaudier pieces, Evelyn Silber, ibid., catalogue nos. 79, 80, 81; for Epstein, Evelyn Silber, *The Sculpture of Epstein with a complete catalogue*, Oxford, 1986, catalogue nos. 48, 50, 53.

17

On a visit to Richmond Park, summer 1914, Gaudier told Sophie Brzeska: 'Nature is really beautiful and interesting to study. It seems after all I should become a naturalist.' In Sophie Brzeska, '*Détails pour Matka*', fols. 149 – 50, Cambridge University Library, Add. Ms 8554, fol 155b (author's translation).

18

T. E. Hulme, draft review of Epstein's first one man show at the Twenty-One Gallery; Tate Gallery Archive TGA 8135, 35.

19

Jon Wood, 'Epstein's Flenite Relief', in James Lomax, Evelyn Silber and Christopher Webster (eds.), *Cornucopia. Essays on architecture, sculpture and the decorative arts in honour of Terry Friedman (1940 – 2013)*, Leeds Art Fund, 2015 (in press).

20

Silber, 1986, no. 42, p. 132, plate 7.

21

From about 1912 until his death in 1959 Epstein formed the finest collection of primitive sculpture in Britain; see Ezio Bassani and Malcolm McLeod, *Jacob Epstein Collector*, Turin, 1989.

22

Sophie Brzeska in '*Détails pour Matka*', fols 149 – 50, Cambridge University Library, Add. Ms fols. 129a, 149 – 50. Her account of attending the London Group show opening confirms Epstein and Gaudier's works were shown together. There remains uncertainty about whether the first or second *Doves* and which of the flenite figures was shown there.

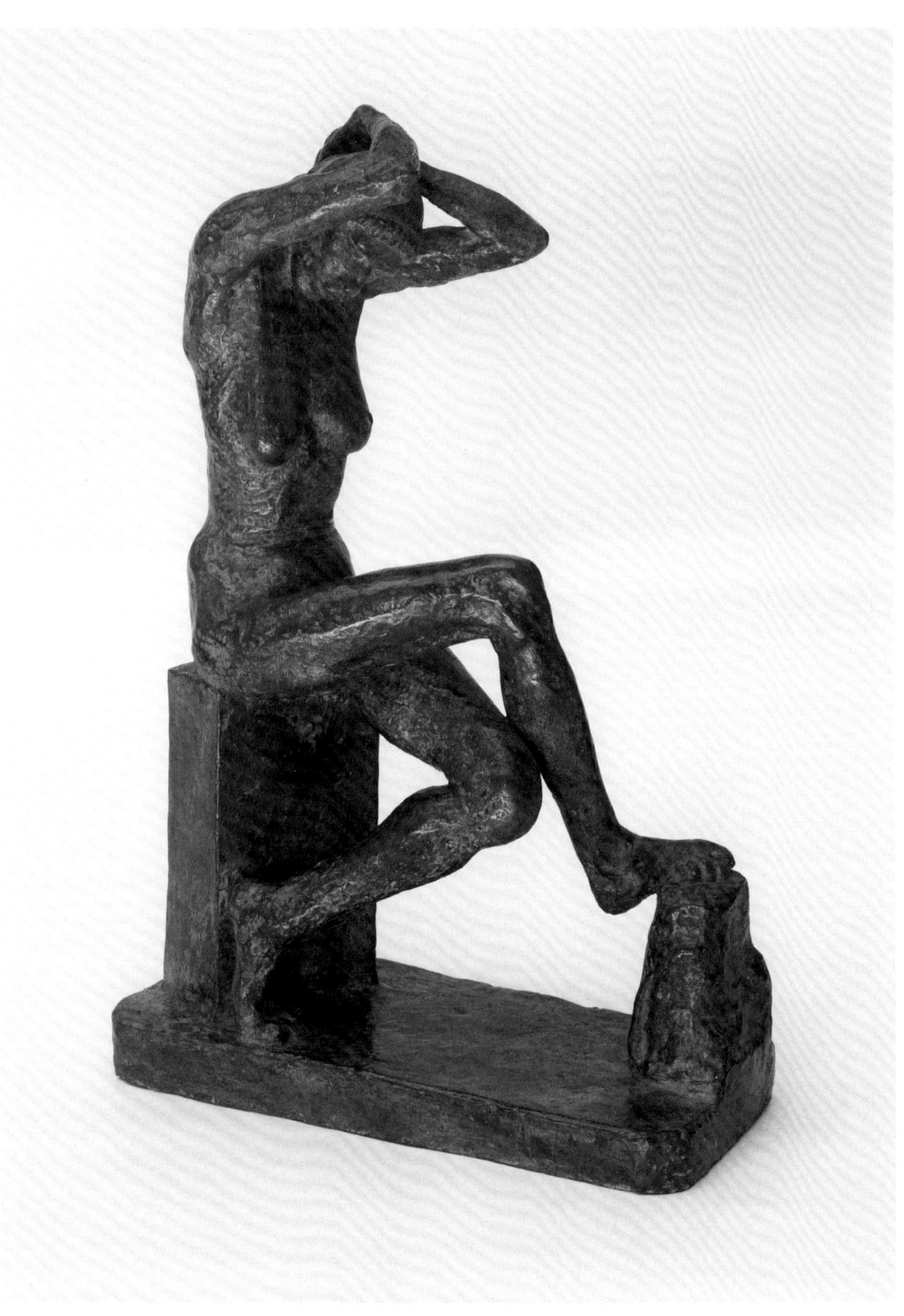

20
Jacob Epstein
Nan Seated, 1910–11

21
Jacob Epstein
Female Figure in Flenite, 1913

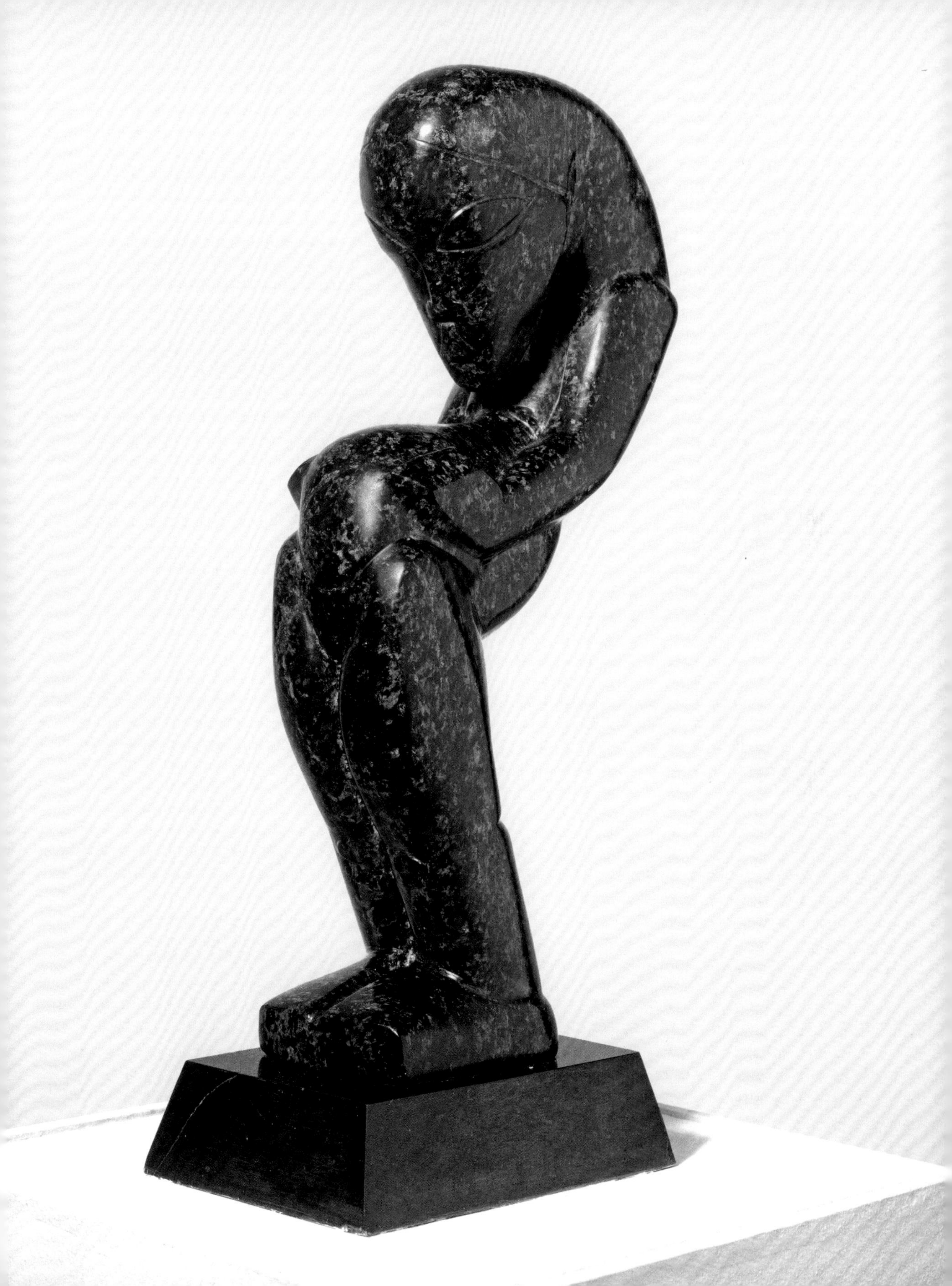

'The model takes his pose – which is, of course, a good thing – and keeps it for ten or fifteen minutes. I should have liked to have a model who didn't pose at all, but did everything he wanted to, walked, ran, danced, sat, etc.'

— Gaudier writing to Sophie Brzeska, 14 November 1912

DRAWING

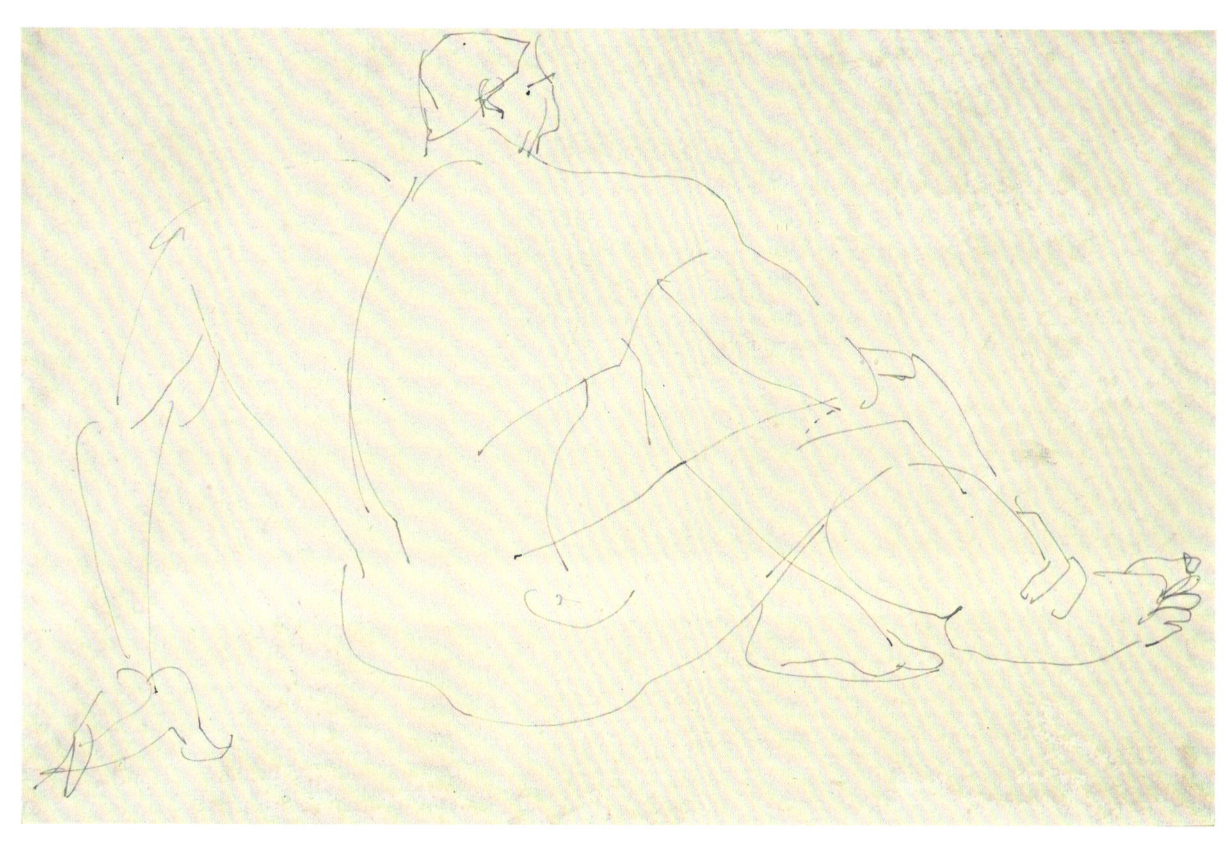

22
Seated male nude, c. 1912 – 3

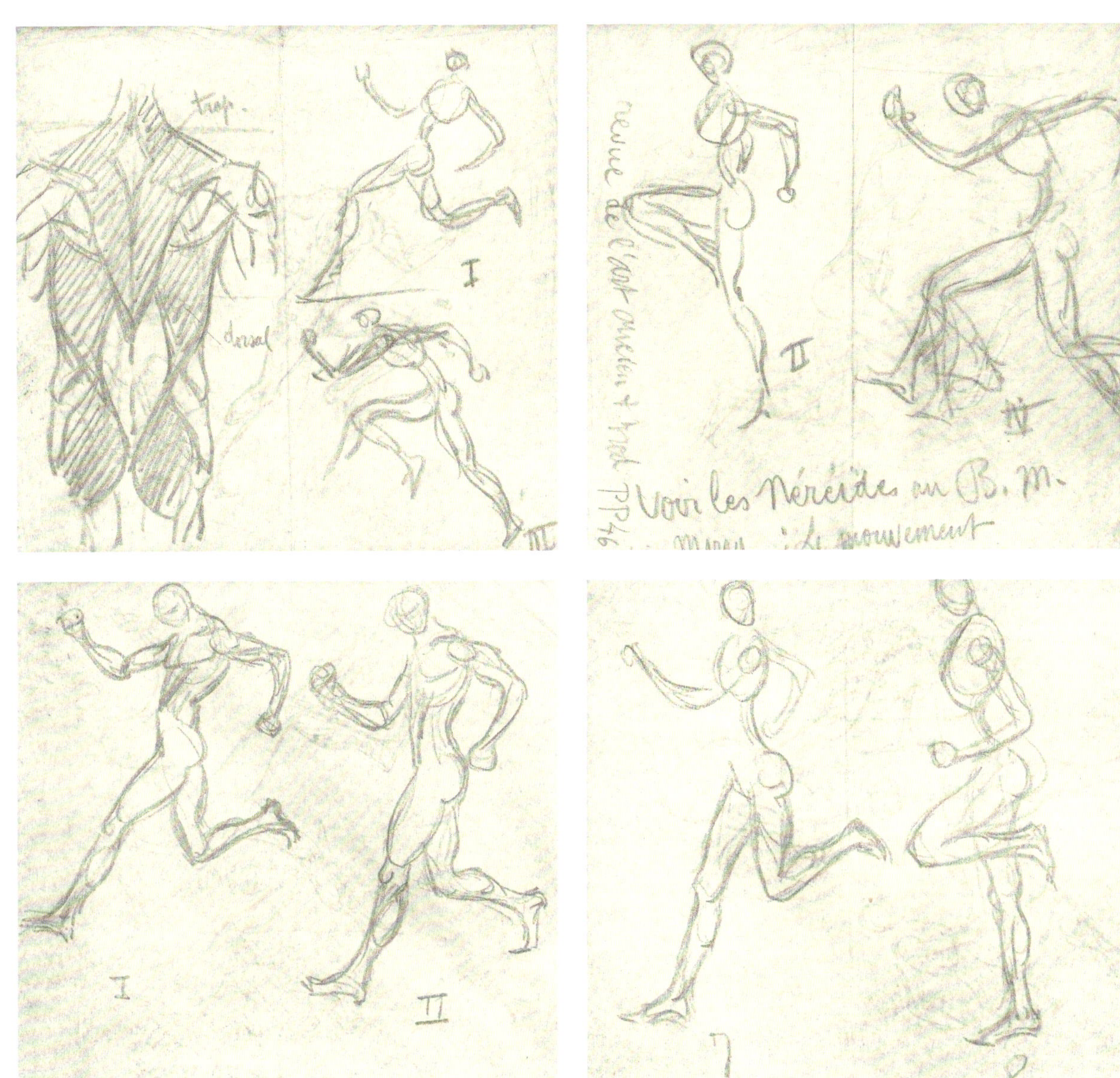

23
Studies of athletes, recto of 4 sheets, c. 1911

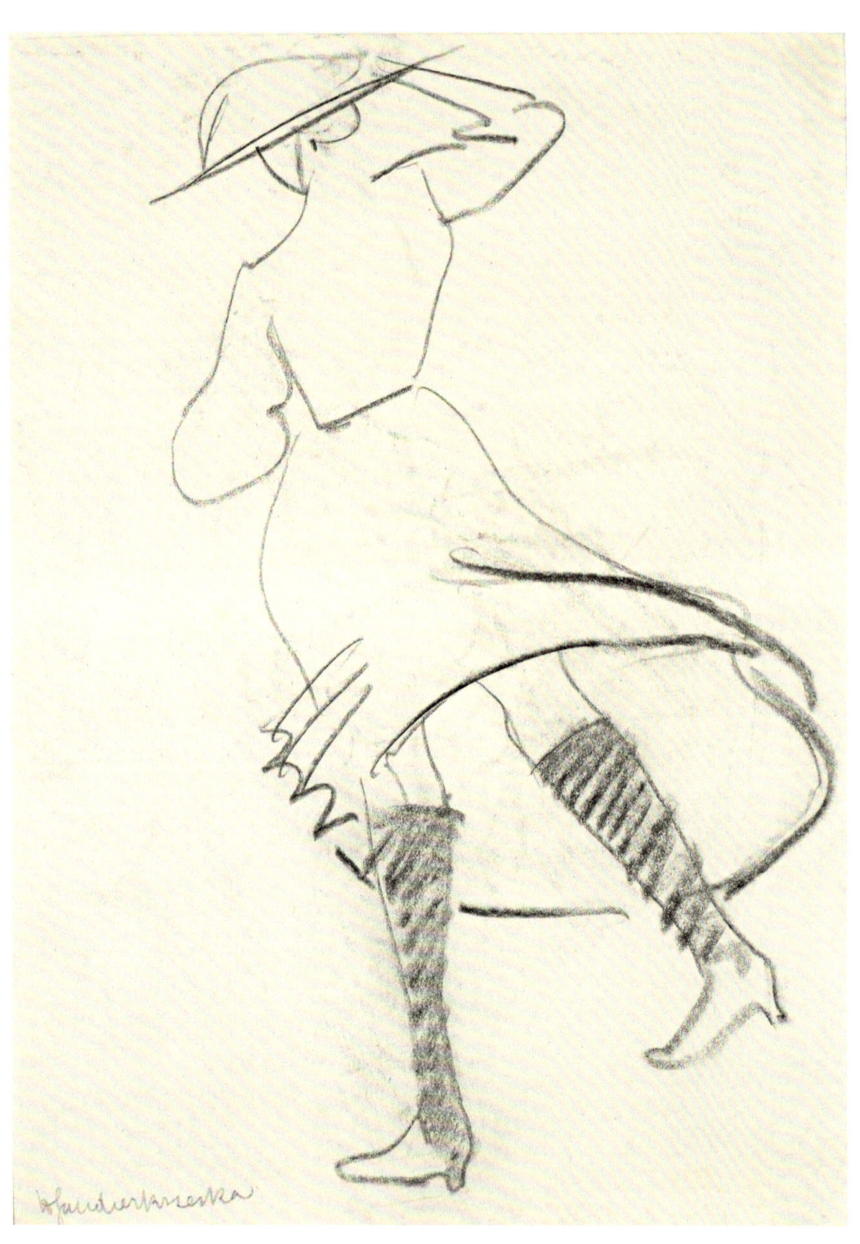

24
Girl with skirt blowing, 1912

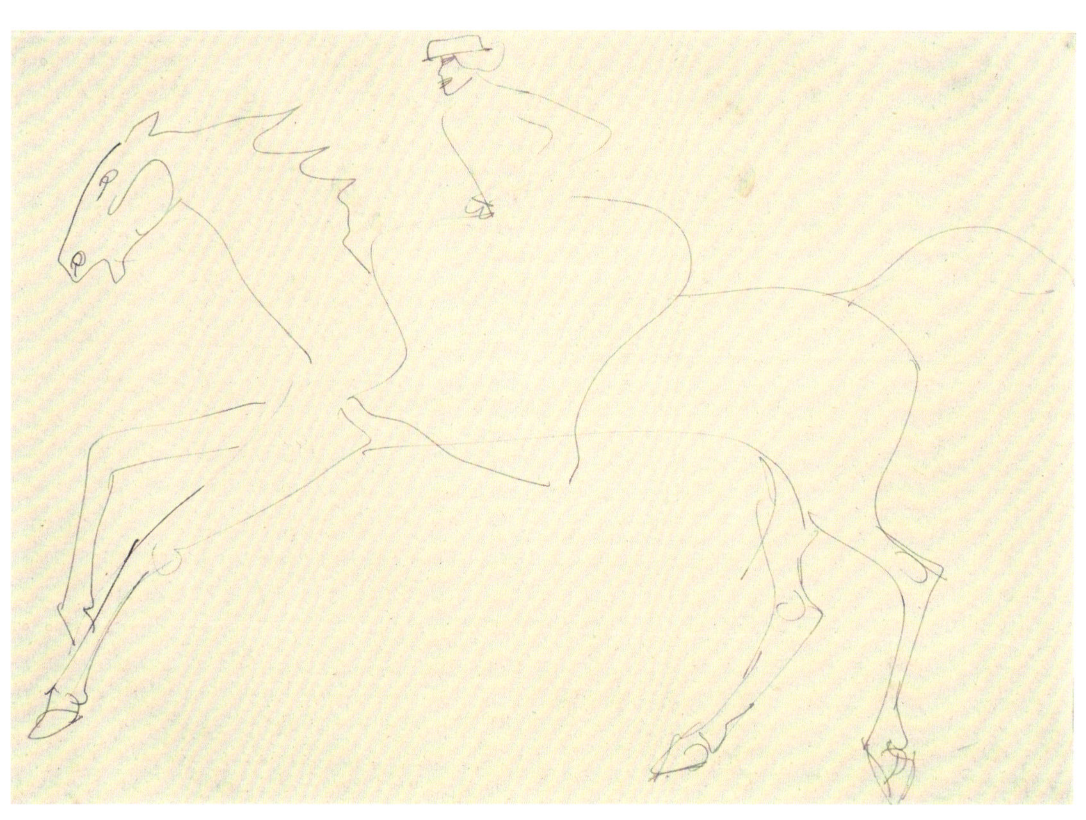

25
Woman on a horse, c. 1912 – 13

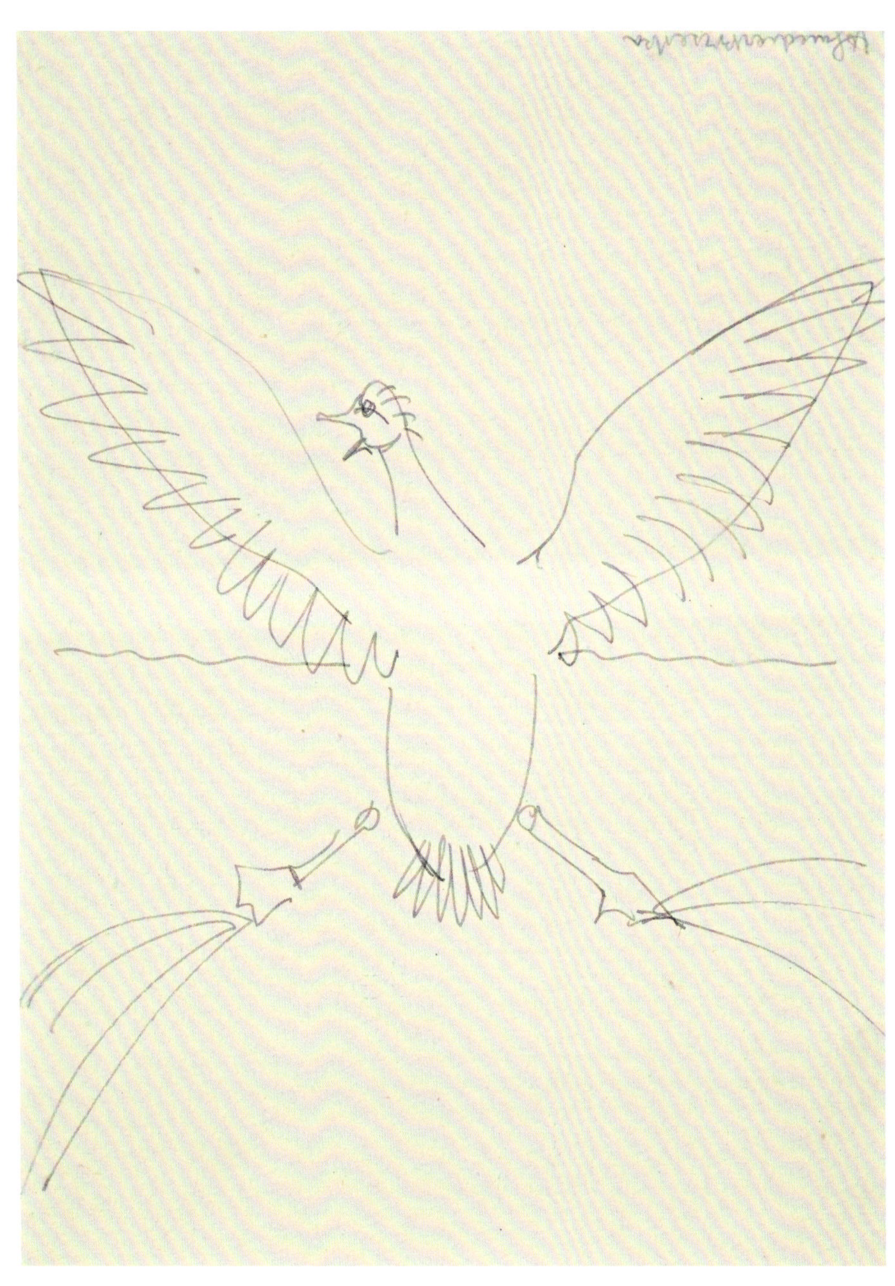

26
Bird landing on water, c. 1912 – 13

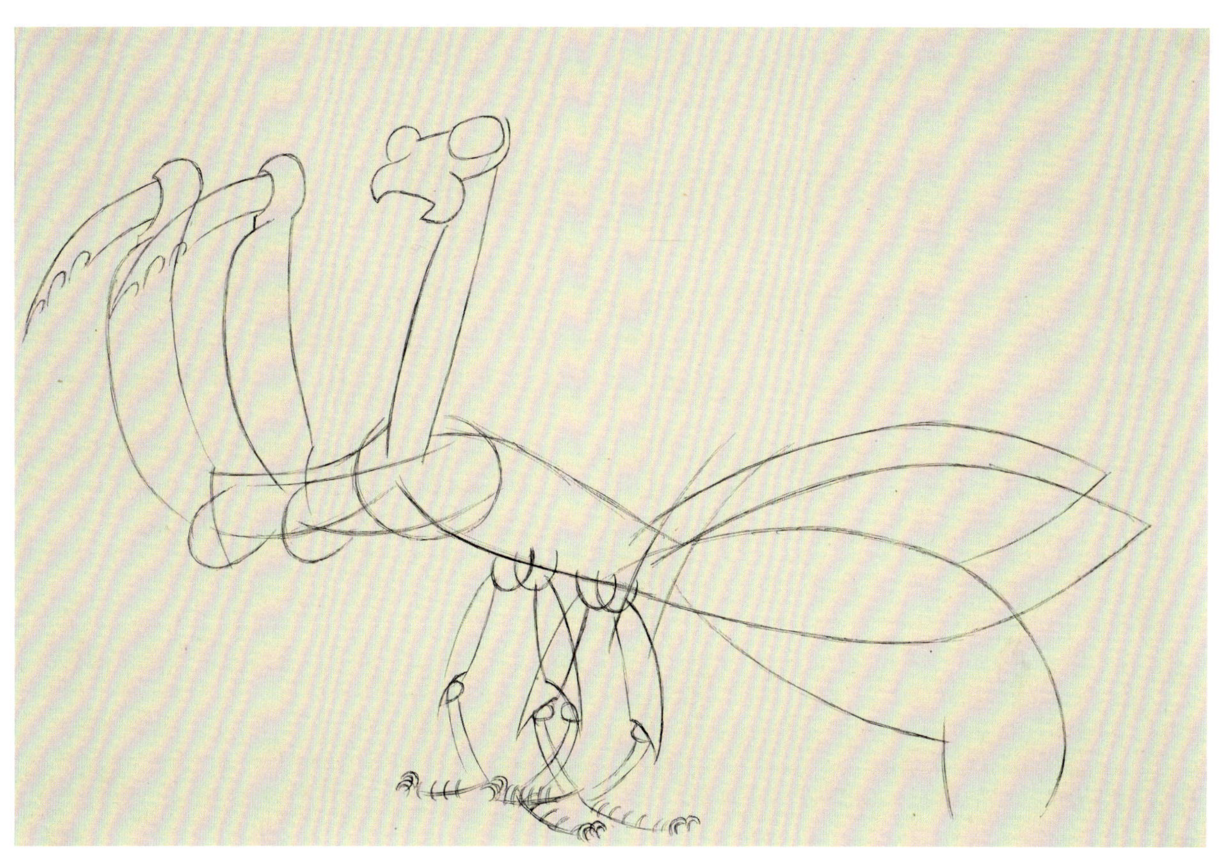

27
Praying Mantis, 1914

'A work of the 'new' art is more likely to result in appreciation, and the aesthetic pleasure which inevitably accompanies these works, than the most strenuous brain-racking, for the senses will immediately seize upon that rhythm of line, harmony of conception, and striking colour which are their greatness.'

— John Rodker in his essay 'The new movement in art', May 1914

CONTEMPORARY RHYTHMS

Sculpture 'Makes us Dance'.
How to Sculpt Dance?

Doïna Lemny (translated by Peter Collier)

Writing in 1954 the Belgian art critic and painter Michel Seuphor drew a parallel between painting ('the easiest of the arts to love. Its colours are crazy little creatures bubbling with lyricism'[1]) and sculpture, a subtler art, more difficult to approach, whose strength lies in its three-dimensional nature, able to suggest and even to involve us in movement and dance: 'We stand stock still when we contemplate a painting, but we move around a sculpture. The one demands contemplation, the other invites our minds rather to wander.' With sculpture, Seuphor continues, 'as we weave around it we change its outline, we change its shadows, and the lines of the sculpture in their turn start to dance. In their dance they compose, decompose, and then recompose their arrangement. This slow displacement of harmonies gradually reveals their qualities, their secret grace and their power.'[2]

Seuphor was writing an introduction to an exhibition of modern sculpture in which there were no figurative depictions of dancers.[3] His interest, as an abstract painter, was in the ways in which modern sculpture can move beyond the pure representation of the body, and encourage our own bodies to move. Constantin Brancusi, whose simplified elongated heads fascinated Henri Gaudier-Brzeska,[4] surrounded himself with dancing girls from the end of the 1910s, but did not represent them in the process of dancing. Rather, their movements inspired Brancusi to push to its limits the ability of sculpture to express lightness, intoxication and ecstasy. He achieves this with his photograph of the sculpture *L'Oiseau dans l'espace* (fig. 18); with the aid of the lighting effects of the camera, this abstract form is captured in the very act of taking flight.

At the end of the nineteenth and beginning of the twentieth-centuries, dance benefited from the wave of freedom that broke through the rigid codes of classical dance. 'La Loïe', as the American artist Loie Fuller (1862–1968) was familiarly known in Paris, embodied this new conception of dance, as she imbued her uncorseted body with natural movement. Her dance was driven by the flowing, lithe movements of her arms, as they unravelled veils of different colours, the flickering tones produced by a careful play of lighting, and sometimes by strategically placed mirrors that created infinite echoes of her image. These new forms of dance and ballet inspired leading sculptors such as Auguste Rodin and Antoine Bourdelle.

Dazzled by the Cambodian dancers who performed with the Royal Cambodian Ballet in Paris in 1906, Rodin wished to capture the kinetic energy of the gestures of these 'magical princesses'.[5] On 8 November 1907, the artist wrote, with some regret, to tell his secretary (the poet Rainer Maria Rilke) of his inability to render the harmonies, the stillness, and the variety of the sequences of set pieces which were executed with such elegance and precision by the Cambodian dancers: 'Despite the urgency of my desire, I was unable to penetrate beneath the surface of this profound and beautiful dance, and I have produced a rather eighteenth-century translation. The Cambodian girls transcend the kind of beauty that I am able – or any of us are able – to grasp.'[6]

The following year, Rodin attended a performance given by the Japanese dancer Hanako. Following this, Rodin asked the dancer to pose regularly for him and produced a number of drawings and masks that were inspired by these encounters. Around 1910, Rodin met the Spanish acrobat and dancer, Alda Moreno, at the Comic Opera. Rodin set out to capture her movements in a long series of drawings. In 1912, the dancer and choreographer Vaslav Nijinsky (1889–1950), whom the sculptor discovered when he attended the second performance

fig. 18
Constantin Brancusi,
L'Oiseau dans l'espace (Bird in Space),
polished bronze 1927, c. 1929–30,
photograph 120 × 90 mm,
Centre Pompidou, MNAM–CCI

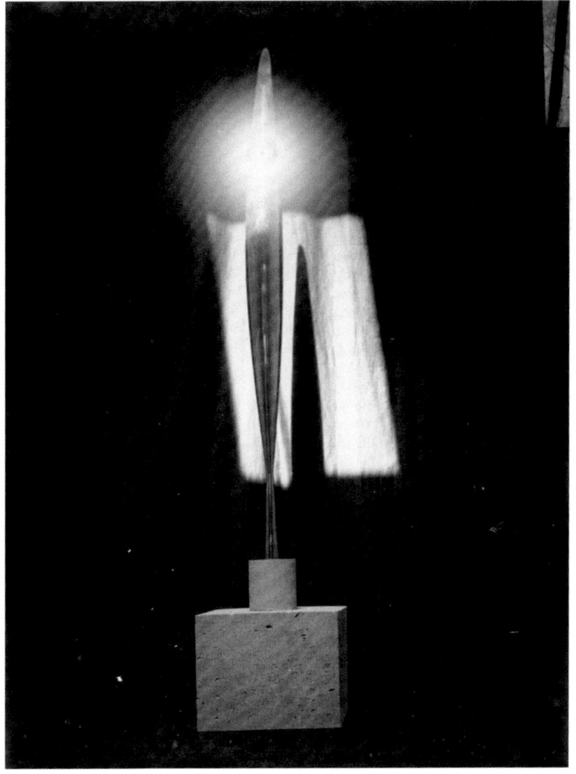

of Claude Debussy's *L'après-midi d'un faune*, agreed to pose
for him. In a small-scale plaster cast representing Nijinski
(c. 1912, cast 1959, pl. 28), Rodin articulates his rotation along
contradictory axes, thus expressing his admiration for a figure
in unpredictable motion: this body, with its urgent thrust
pivoting around a fragile axis, is a fusion of dynamically
developing tensions – as much those of the dancer as the
sculptor. A series of nine small-scale terracotta *Dance Movements*
(c. 1911, cast 1950s, pl. 30) bear witness to the sculptor's desire
to capture in sequence the harmony of the dancers' bodies
and their transformation through action and over time.
Rodin's challenge was to express through sculpture the
elusive essence of this interlocking chain of 'successive
but motionless postures'.

With Isadora Duncan (1877–1927), dance crossed another
threshold towards a freer liberation of the body and emotional
expression through movement. When Rodin met Duncan in
1908, at the time when he was moving into the Hôtel Biron,[7]
he discovered a kind of 'classical antiquity' in the perfection
of her natural positions, her spontaneous movements and the
purity of her gestures, usually expressed through the
transparent veils that she wore. Rodin's contemporary, the
French sculptor Antoine Bourdelle (1861–1929), was equally
bewitched by Isadora Duncan. Her elegant and natural step
as she moved, often barefoot over grass, and her slow, sweeping,
turning movements creating curves and spirals in space
recalled, for Bourdelle, forms from Ancient Greece. In response
the artist was inspired to create what might be described as
a calligraphy of gesture, which he transposed onto paper, in
a manner reminiscent of Rodin's previous series of over fifty
drawings of dancers. Bourdelle used these drawings as the
groundwork for bas reliefs, in which he alternated full and
empty forms, following the natural rhythms of the dancer.
One of the five metopes that he sculpted in 1911–12 for the
frieze of the Theatre of the Champs-Elysées, presents a
dramatic and rhythmic interweaving of dancers' forms (fig. 19).

The enthusiasm of these two sculptors for the metamorphosis
of the ballet into a liberated dance went no further: they never
again created sculptures deriving from their relation to this
ephemeral art. Rodin's admission of his inability to render the
subtlety and the beauty of the movements of the dancer's body
reflects a timeless challenge. How can the sculptor, judging
the weight of his material in relation to the lightness and
the spontaneity of the gesture he wishes to render, transcend
the resistance that the density of the marble, plaster or metal
presents to the mobility expressed through dance? Sculptors
such as Alexander Archipenko in his *Dance* (1912) and

28
Auguste Rodin
Nijinsky, 1912,
bronze cast 1959

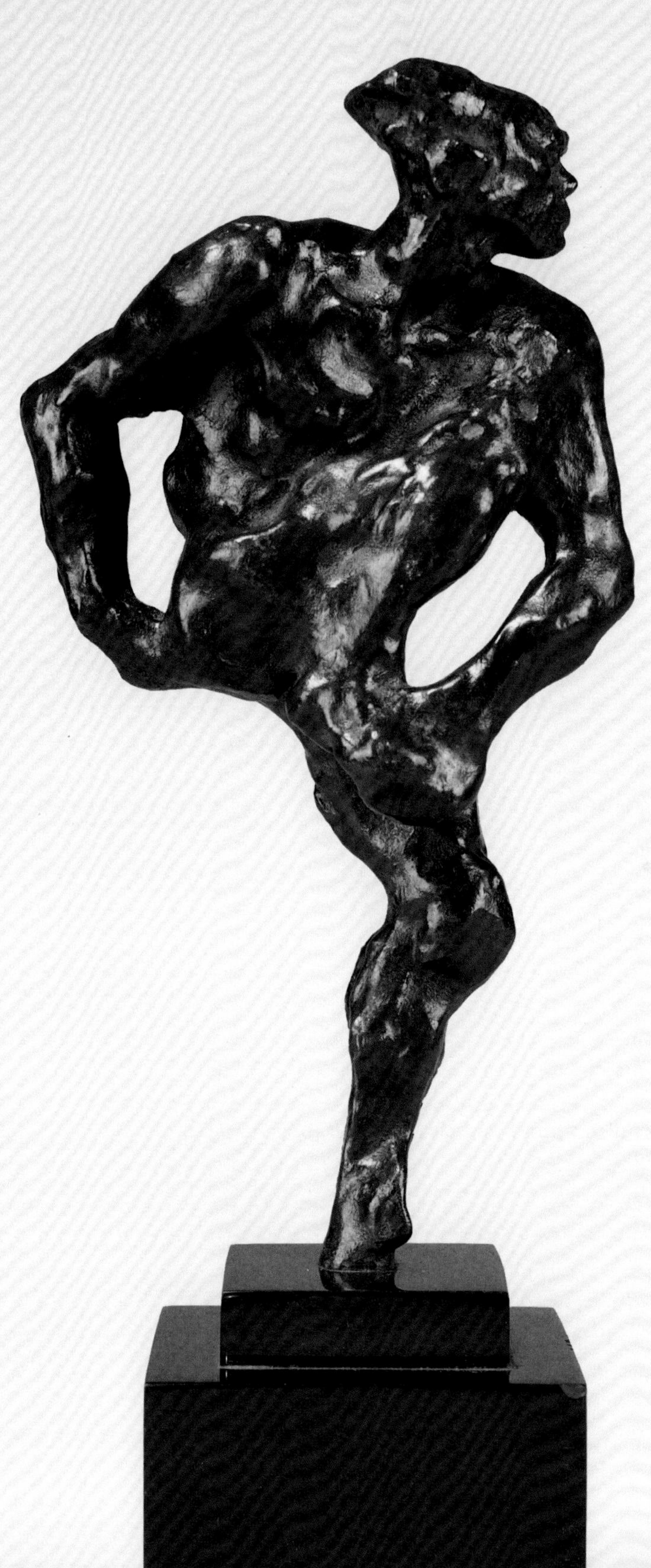

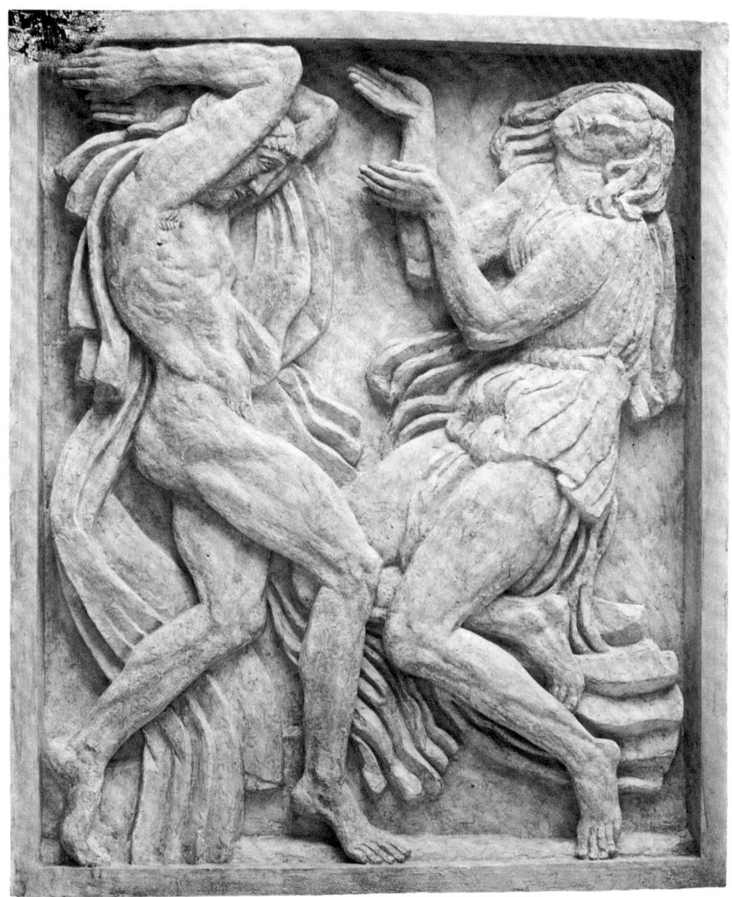

Blue Dancer (1913, private collection) and Gaudier in his
The Firebird (1912, pls. 4, 5) and *The Dancer* (1913, pls. 6, 7),
experimented with this fragile balancing act between the
harmony of the body and the twists and turns of the dance.

The Dancer (pls. 6, 7), for which Nina Hamnett posed,[8] preserves
that fluidity of motion and elegance of the undulating body.
Gaudier attempted to disperse its masses into a circular pattern
around a central void, releasing a whirling energy. With *Red
Stone Dancer* (c. 1913–14, pls. 8, 9), the artist went on to free
himself from depicting the anatomy, by distorting the parts of
the body as a function of the twisting motion that he imposed
on the silhouette. Gaudier emphasises his satisfaction with the
beauty of this piece, probably because it is the incarnation of
his research into techniques of the deconstruction of volumes
(notably those of the human body), and the interplay between
positive and negative space, and because it displays his
ability to endow each of these masses with the impression
of movement.[9]

Where Archipenko, in his *The Dance* (1912 – 13, pl. 39) translated the movement and the rhythm of the body using fragmentary forms, Gaudier in *Red Stone Dancer* follows the movement through by framing it within clearly defined geometrical registers. Thus the spiral evoked by the pivoting of the body around the left foot drives the interplay of the intertwining elements of the torso into an unnatural movement: the right arm stretches round to its furthest limit as it clasps the left shoulder, framing the upper mass in a triangle, re-emphasised in its turn by the triangle of the schematic face. The left hand, placed discreetly between the two breasts, which are each accentuated by a different geometric figure, leads this spiral into a bolder, more continuous and serpentine curve. Through these interlacing forms, in coinciding instances of creating and unravelling, Gaudier finally transcribes the complex movement of dance. As Seuphor describes in the introductory quotation, this sculpture makes us move.

1
Michel Seuphor, 'Sept pionniers de la sculpture moderne', Yverdon, 1954, unpaged.

2
Ibid.

3
The artists included in the exhibition were Henri Laurens, Raymond Duchamp-Villon, Constantin Brancusi, Jean Arp, Jean-Gabriel Chauvin, Antoine Pevsner, and Julio González.

4
Three of these heads were exhibited at the Allied Artists' Salon exhibition of 1913. Gaudier's work was also included in the exhibition.

5
Fragment of a letter from Rodin to Rilke on 8 November 1907, cited in Hugues Herpin, 'Et la sculpture?' in *Rodin et les danseuses cambodgiennes. Sa dernière passion*, Paris, 2006, p. 75.

6
Ibid.

7
The Hôtel Biron, which in that year housed Cocteau, Matisse, Rodin and the actor Édouard de Max, became the Rodin Museum in 1919.

8
Nina Hamnett, *Laughing Torso*, New York, 1932, p. 38.

9
Red Stone Dancer is listed in Gaudier's 'list of works', Kettle's Yard Collection, as 'poli à la cire' (waxed), Kettle's Yard. Reproduced in *Henri Gaudier-Brzeska*, Centre Pompidou, Paris, 2009, p. 187.

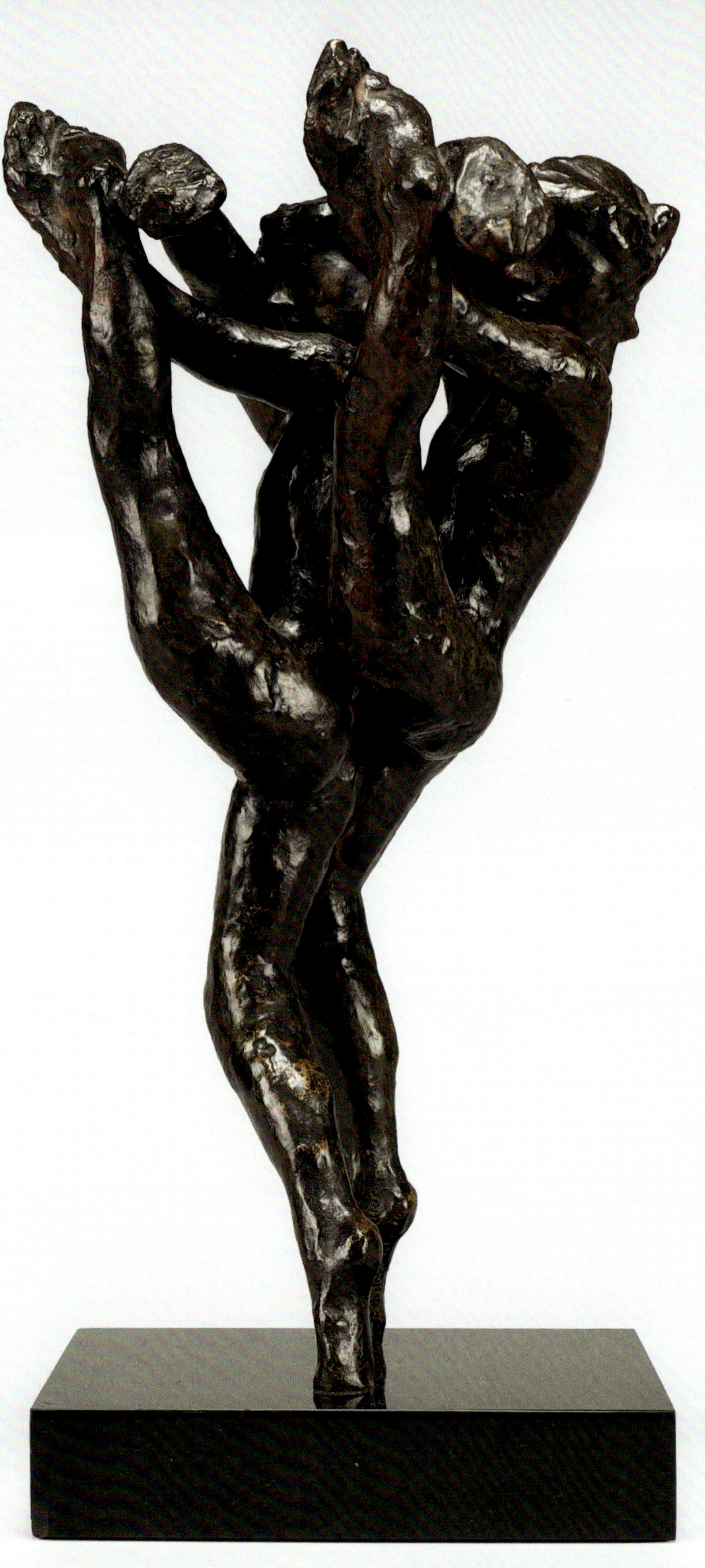

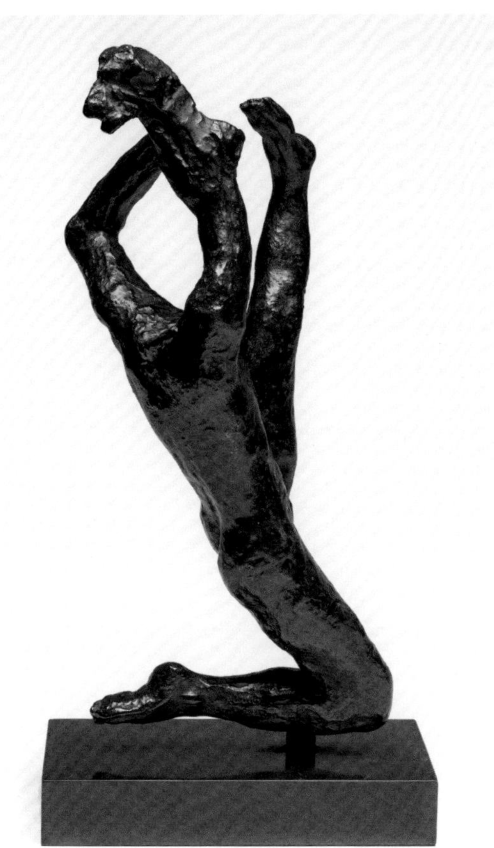

29
Auguste Rodin
Pas-de-Deux, Study Type B, 1911,
bronze cast 1964

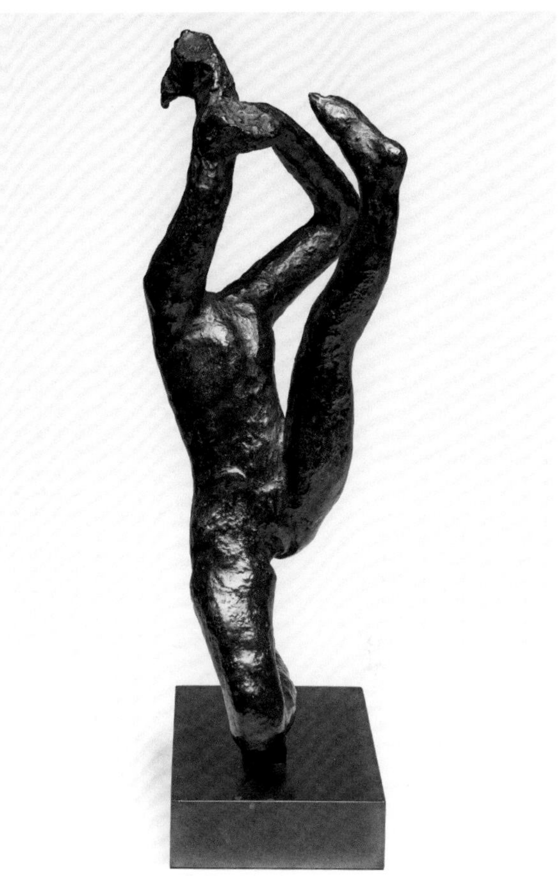

30
Auguste Rodin
Dance Movement H, c. 1911,
bronze cast c. 1950s

31
William Roberts
The Toe Dancer, 1914

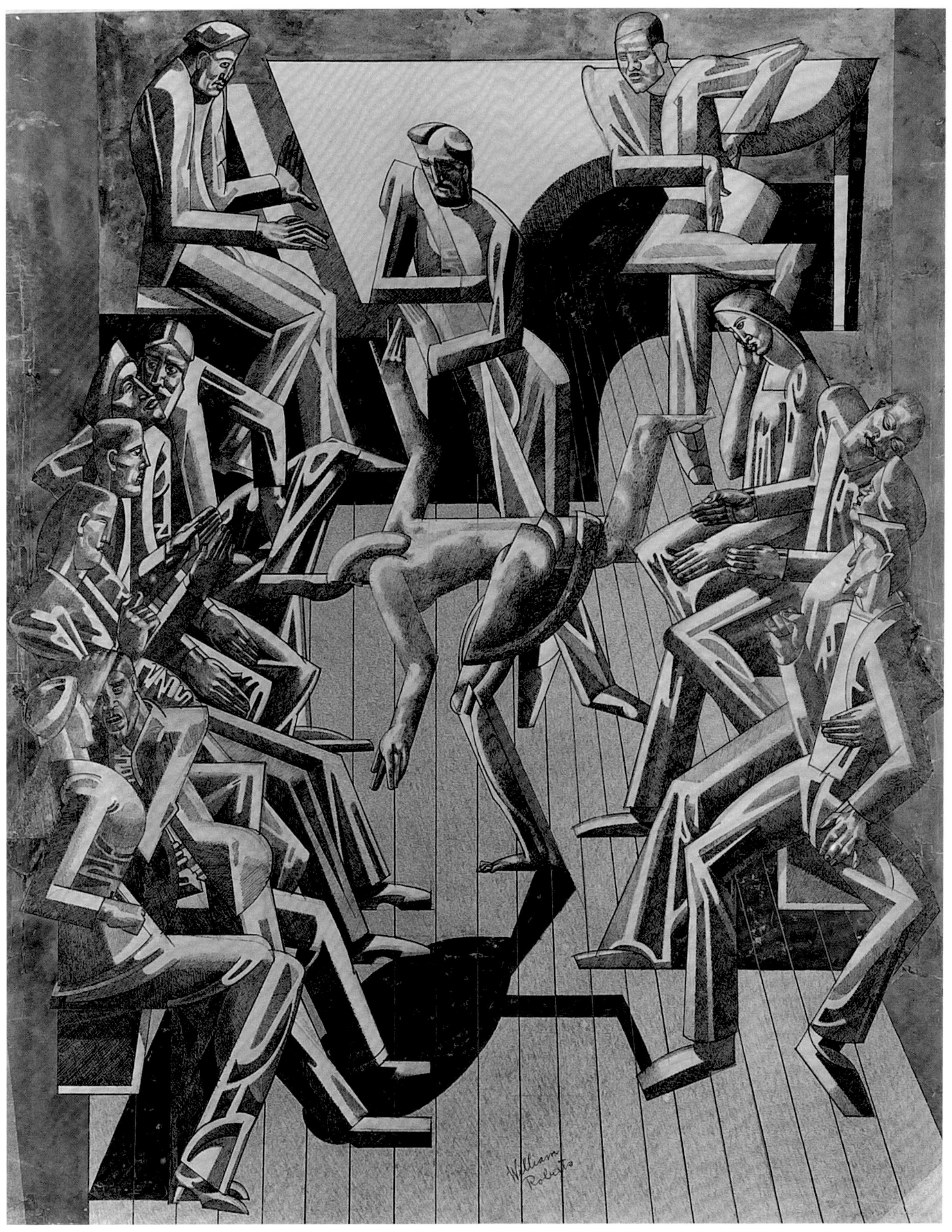

William
Roberts

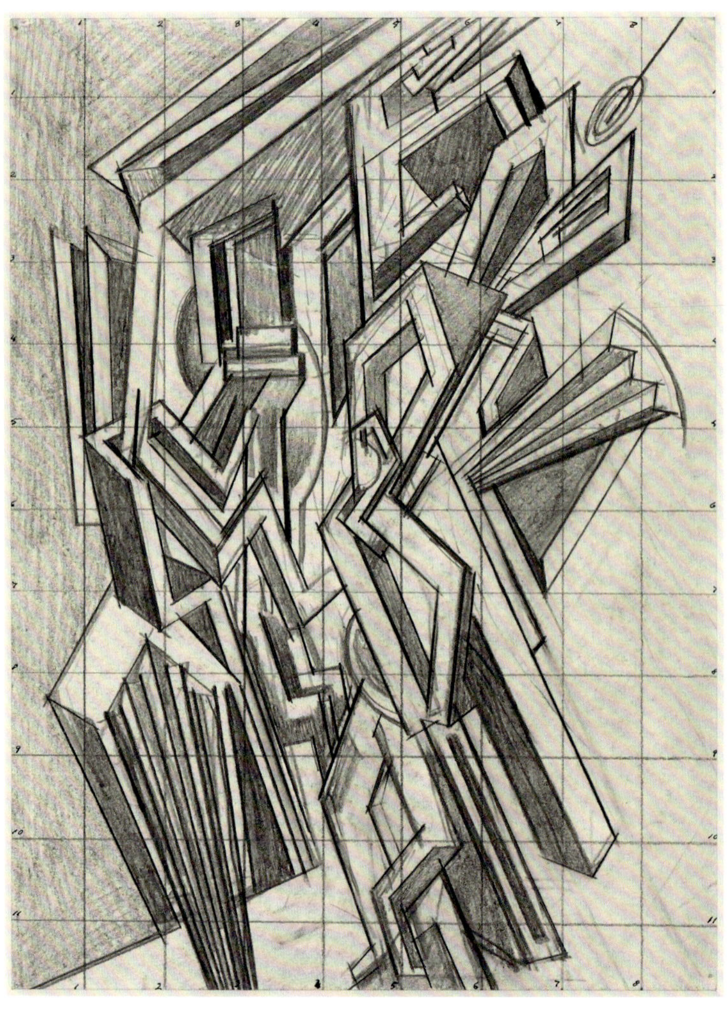

32
William Roberts
Study for Two Step, 1915

33
William Roberts
*Study for the lost painting Two-Step;
abstract design with orange and green
background*, 1915

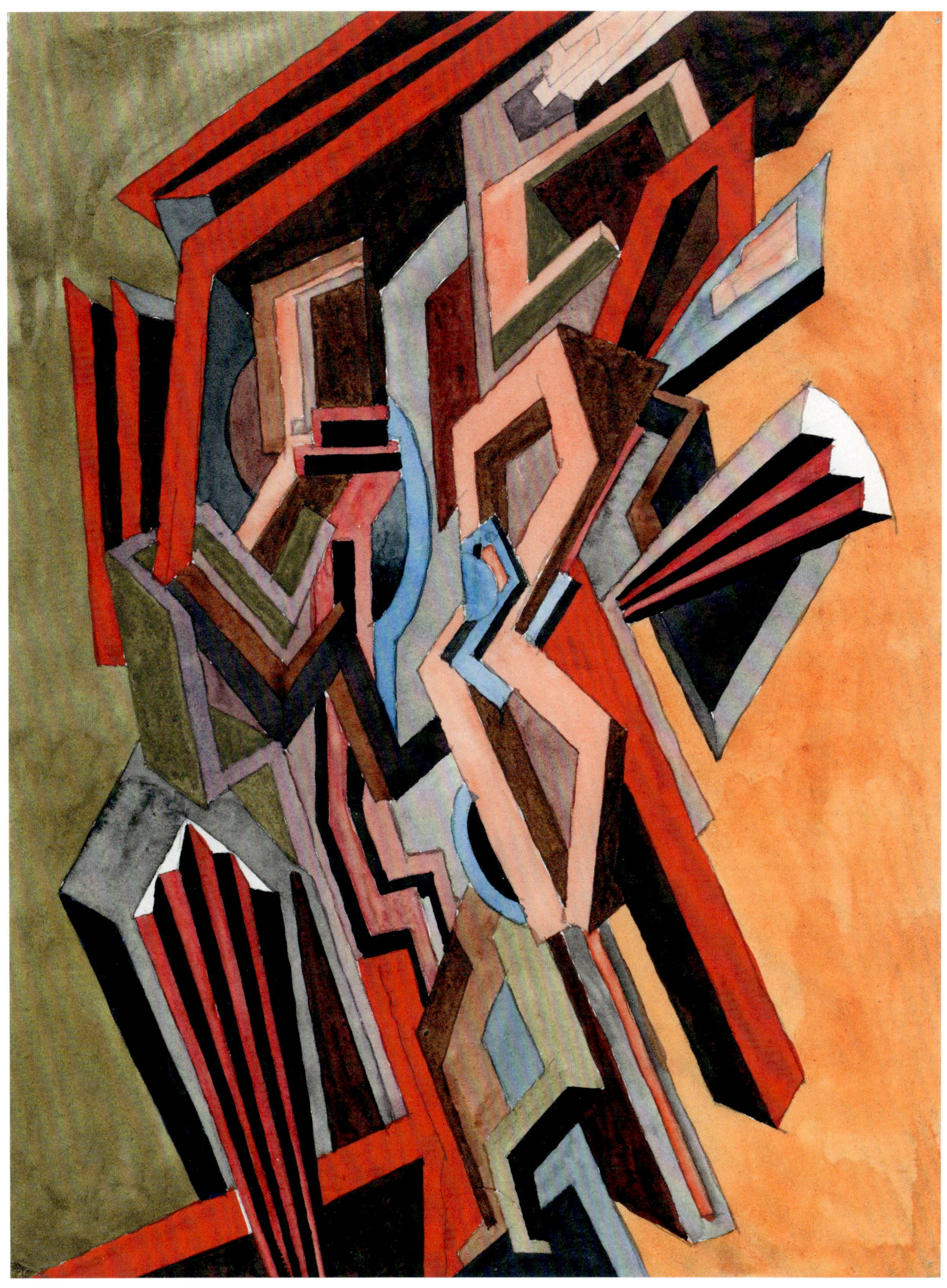

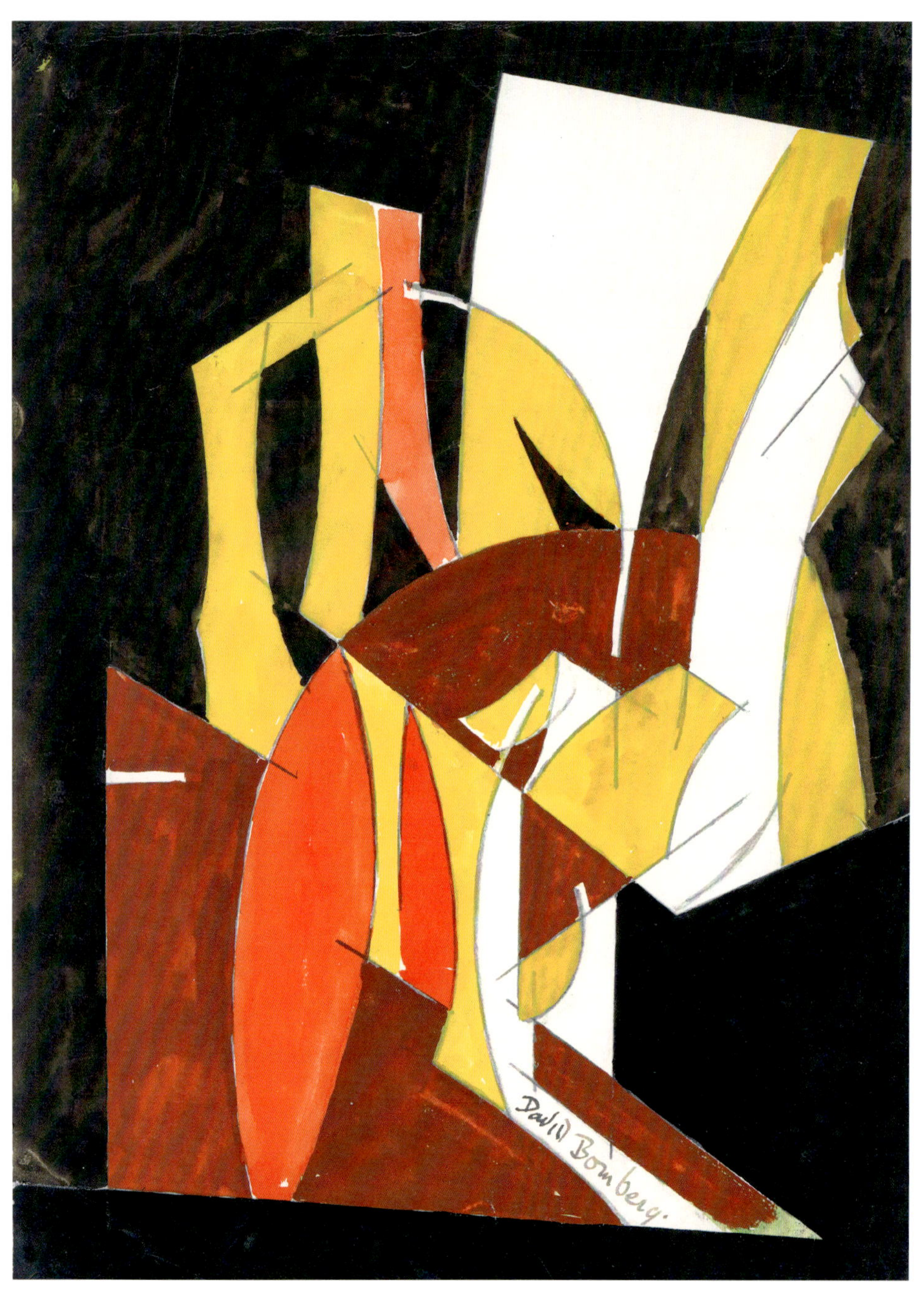

34
David Bomberg
The Dancer, abstract design in red,
yellow, brown and blue, c. 1913 – 14

35
David Bomberg
The Dancer, c. 1913 – 14

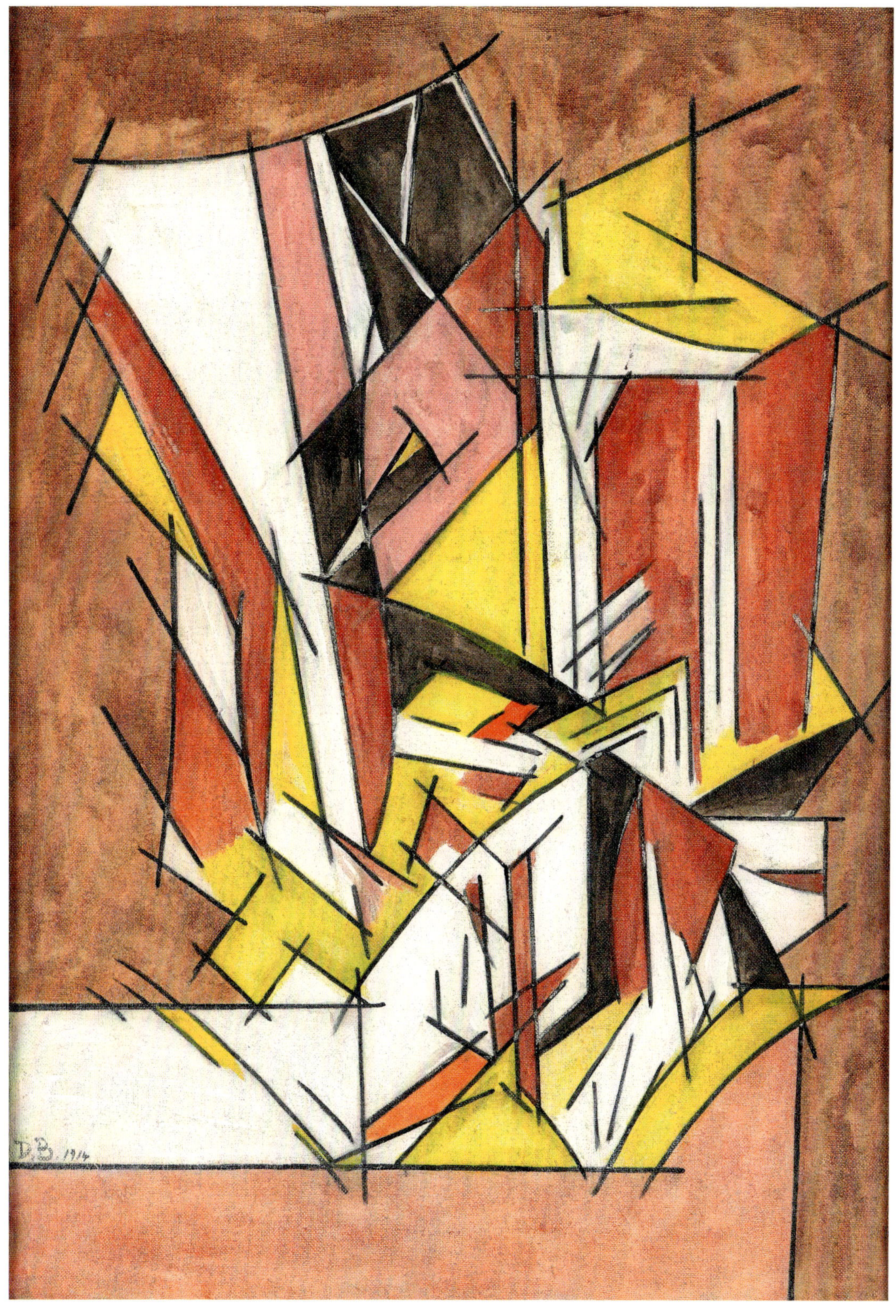

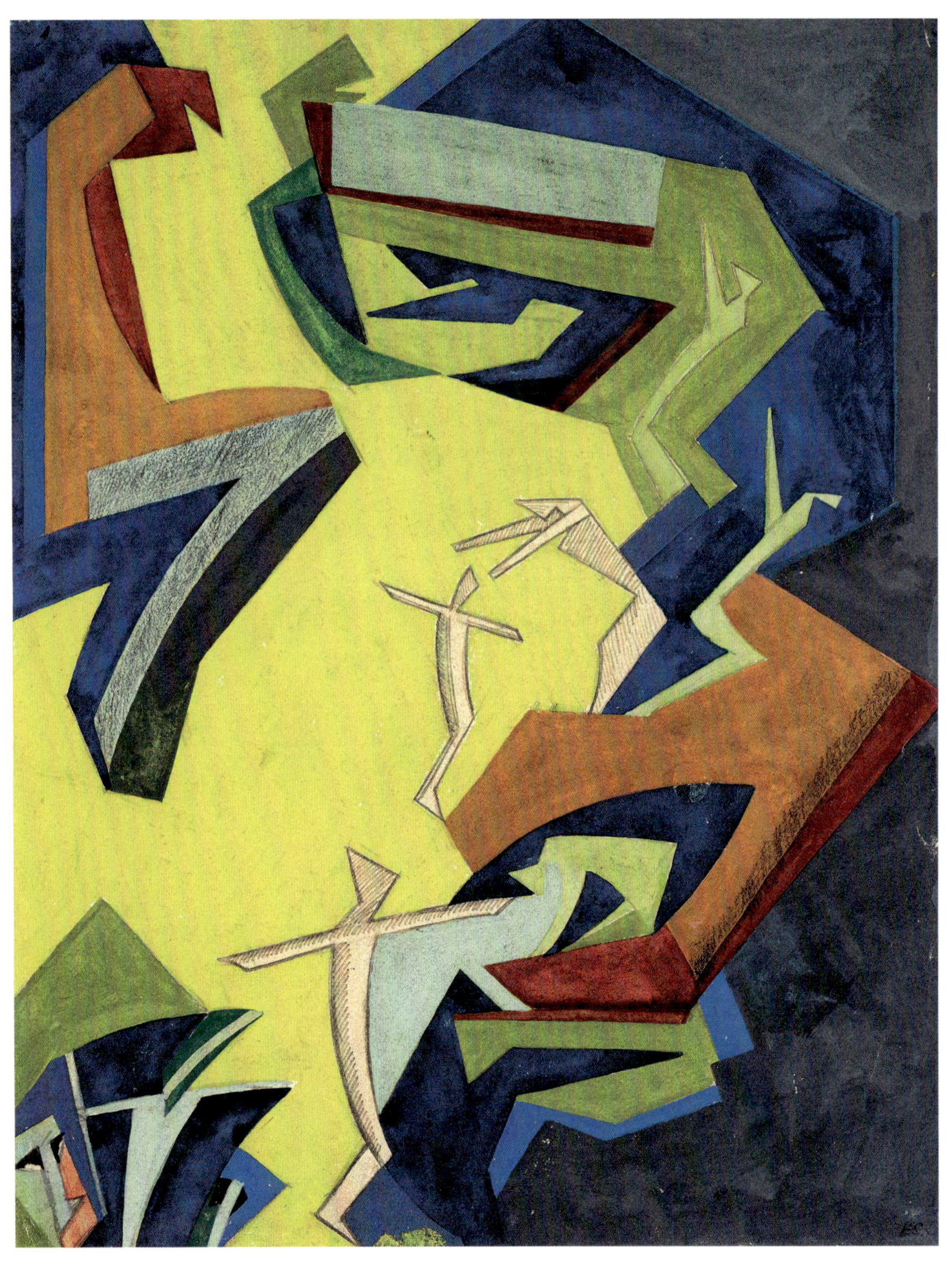

36
Helen Saunders
*Vorticist Composition
in green or yellow*, c. 1915

37
Helen Saunders
Cabaret, c. 1913–14

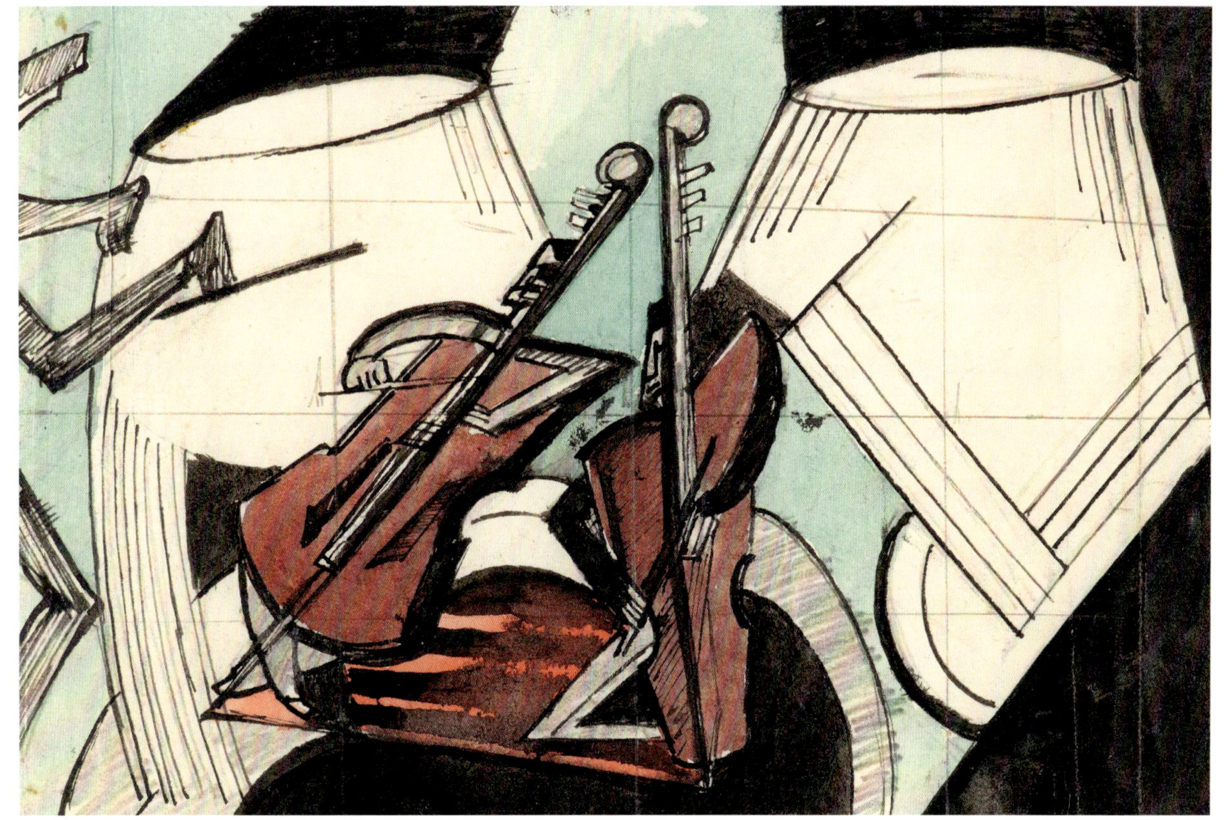

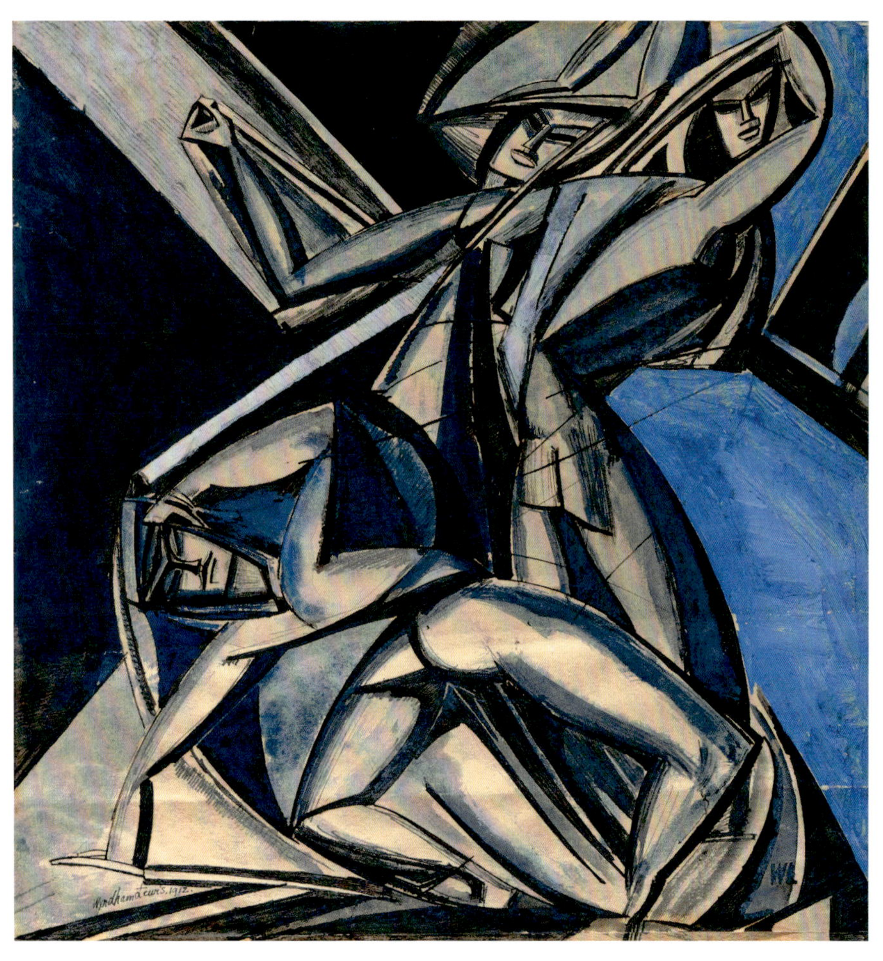

38
Percy Wyndham Lewis
The Dancers (Study for Kermesse), 1912

39
Alexander Archipenko
The Dance, 1912–13,
bronze cast 1959

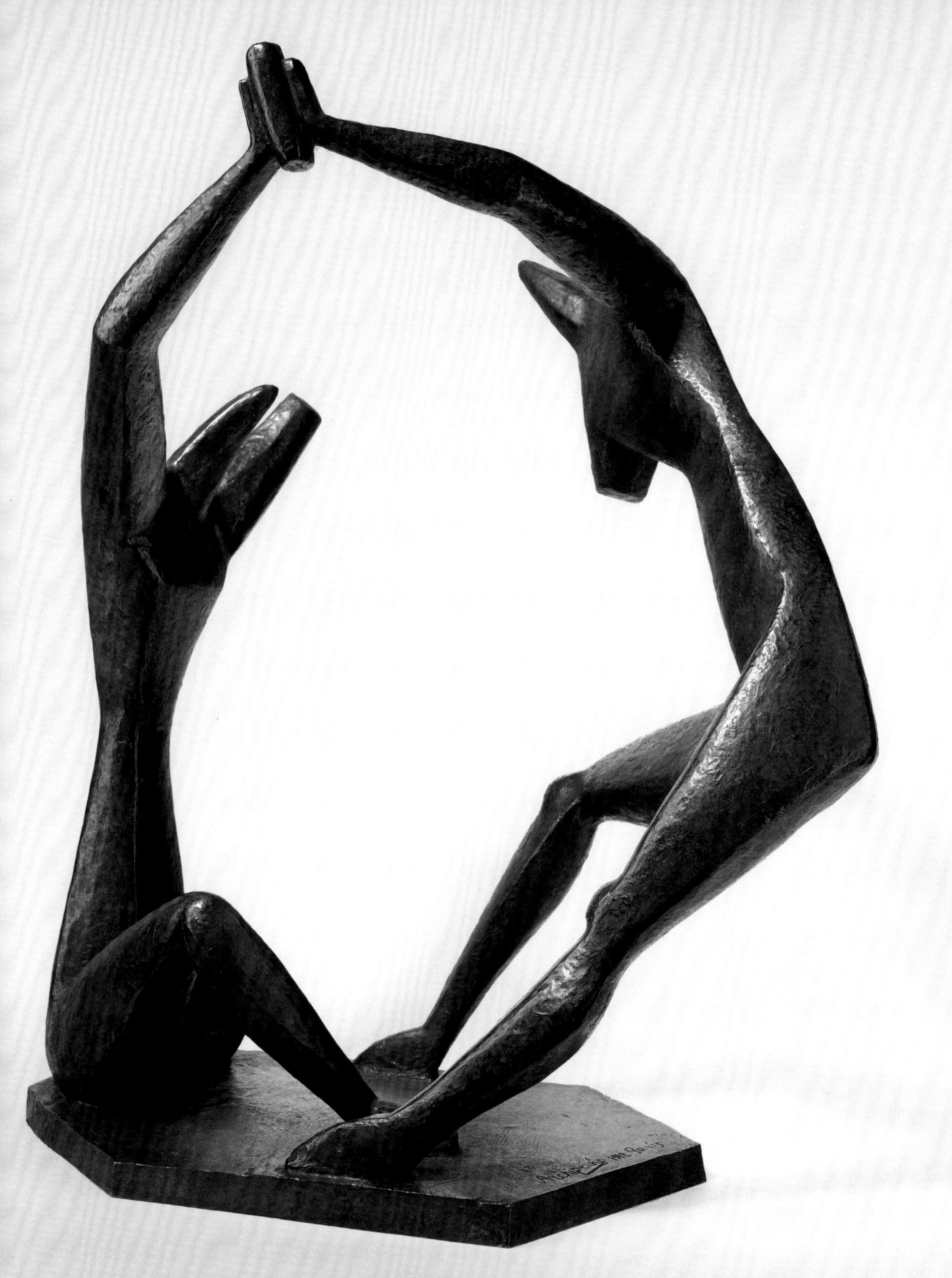

'Last night I went to see the wrestlers – God!
I have seldom seen anything so lovely [...].
They fought with amazing vivacity and spirit,
turning in the air, falling back on their heads,
and in a flash they were up again on the other
side, utterly incomprehensible.'

— Gaudier writing to Sophie Brzeska, 5 December 1912

WRESTLING

A 'Knot of Violent Living':
Henri Gaudier-Brzeska's Wrestlers

Sarah Victoria Turner

'So the two men entwined and wrestled with each other, working nearer and nearer. Both were white and clear […] So they wrestled swiftly, rapturously, intent and mindless at last, two essential white figures working into a tighter closer oneness of struggle, with a strange, octopus-like knotting and flashing of limbs in the subdued light of the room; a tense white knot of flesh gripped in silence between the walls of old brown books […] Often, in the white interlaced knot of violent living being that swayed silently, there was no head to be seen, only the swift, tight limbs, the solid white backs, the physical junction of two bodies clinched into oneness.'[1]

These are D. H. Lawrence's words, describing with a fulsome physicality of their own, the naked wrestling bouts in the evocatively-titled "Gladiatorial" chapter between Gerald Crich and Rupert Birkin, the male protagonists of his 1920 novel *Women in Love*. Reading this passage after looking at Henri Gaudier-Brzeska's plaster sculptural *Wrestlers relief* (1913–14, cast 1965, pl. 49), the resemblances between Lawrence's literary wrestling match and Gaudier's two grappling wrestlers are striking. The 'strange, octopus-like knotting', the 'tense white knot' and the 'physical junction of two bodies clinched into oneness' of Crich and Birkin's tussle also describe perfectly the tangle of the sculpted limbs that Gaudier carved from white plaster. Lawrence's description stresses that there is a daring aesthetics to wrestling, a certain frisson, which stems from the visual relationship of two bodies in close proximity; a proximity which has the potential to destabilise physical boundaries when limbs wrap into tense knots of flesh and muscle, often making it difficult to ascertain where one body ends and another begins. This certainly happens to the right-hand side of the *Wrestlers relief*. Hands, forearms, elbows, upper thighs and lower calves tangle into a 'white interlaced knot' (fig. 40) to such an extent that it almost becomes an abstract pattern of form. Locked in a hold on the white plaster ground, Gaudier's two wrestling bodies sway silently for a moment, their elongated backs and long limbs curving and looping around and over one another.[2]

Lawrence may have seen Gaudier's *Wrestlers relief* when it was exhibited in public for the first time in 1918 at the memorial exhibition of Gaudier's work at the Leicester Galleries in London, organised by the sculptor's friend and collaborator, the poet Ezra Pound (Lawrence was revising *Women in Love* for publication at this time). Whether he did or not, what is certain is that wrestling, combat and violent sport more broadly, became a subject of some fascination within early twentieth-century artistic and literary avant-garde circles. Boxing held particular allure for Gaudier's fellow Vorticists Wyndham Lewis and William Roberts, as Bernard Vere has recently examined.[3] Prior to carving the *Wrestlers relief*, Gaudier had tackled another combative subject in 1911 with his poster design for Black & White scotch whisky (pl. 42). Every muscle on the bodies of these fighters is exaggeratedly taught, rippling under the force of the fierce punch and blow: these men are modern Hercules (a figure that Gaudier had also drawn and sculpted), gladiators for a modern world. The accompanying slogan 'THIS WAS A GREAT FIGHT BETWEEN BLACK & WHITE' suggests that Gaudier followed the media storm surrounding the 1910 fight between 'Jack' Johnson and James Jackson Jeffries, a black and a white boxer, which was widely touted as the fight of the century for the American Heavyweight Championship or, perhaps, the cancelled match between Johnson and Bombardier Billy Wells. Significantly, 1911 was the year in which a colour bar was introduced into British boxing.[4]

40
Wrestlers relief (detail),
c. 1913–14, herculite cast 1965

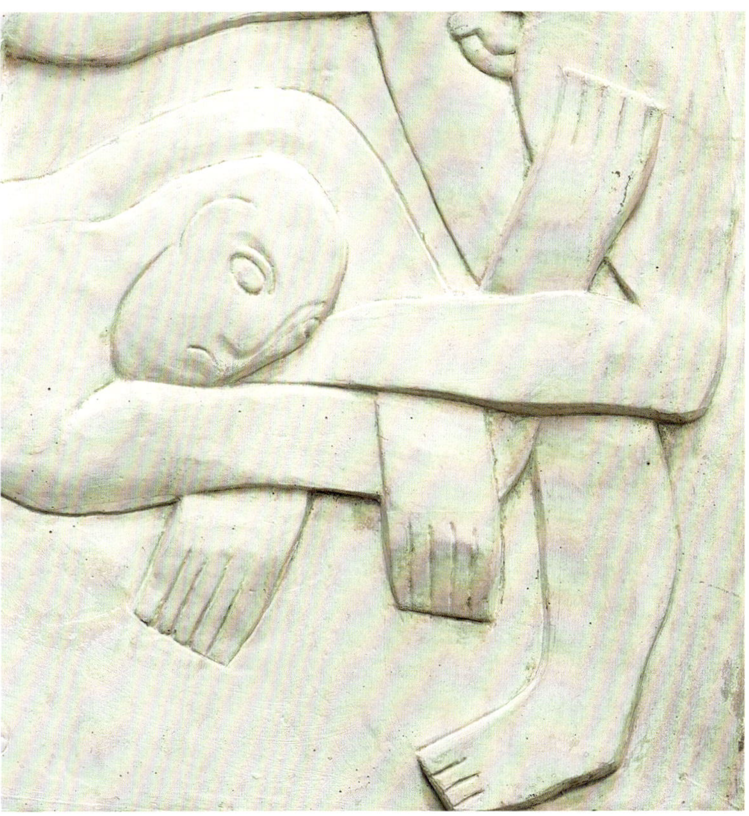

Enjoying huge popularity at the beginning of the twentieth century, photographs and mass reproduced images of both boxing and wrestling featured frequently in the press, as well as on posters and advertising, easily visible in early twentieth-century London. The *Times* reported in 1911 that there had recently been a 'remarkable revival of interest in boxing and wrestling; and the contests between professional experts are watched by large gatherings of spectators.'[5] Sporting contests associated with international exhibitions of the period, including the arrival of a large delegation of Japanese sumo wrestlers for displays at the Anglo-Japan exhibition at White City in 1910, also encouraged interest in the sport and emphasised that Greco-Roman was not wrestling's only lineage. Gaudier's depictions of naked wrestlers suggests that the artist was aware of wrestling styles from other parts of the world – an interest that can also be connected to his wider inquisitiveness about the arts and rituals of other cultures, especially those of Asia and Africa, which he sustained through visits to the collections of major museums in Paris and London.[6]

Gaudier certainly drew on mass media imagery of the wrestling 'revival' when developing his visual vocabulary of the fighting body, but there were also other, closer encounters with wrestlers and wrestling which had a deep impact on the young sculptor. Having never been to art school, Gaudier enrolled at life drawing classes on 12 November 1912. They offered the artist access to life models, including one that he described to his partner Sophie Brzeska as 'the very wrestler that I like so much – a wonderful boy, strong, taut, and finely square'.[7] Inspired by such up-close access, Gaudier drew at a furious rate, telling Sophie that he came away with 150 to 200 drawings from one session compared to what he regarded as the paltry two or three of his fellow classmates. His drawing of a very toned male nude (pl. 41) – 'strong, taut, and finely square' – with one arm raised in a pose conventional to the repertoire of the life class suggest that this was executed when the wrestler was presented for the students to draw.[8] The contours of the body and its key muscle groups are outlined simply and effectively with an economy of line. It is a rapid sketch, but an observant one which manages to convey incredible power and strength through a few lines.

There were other opportunities for drawing athletes and wrestlers too besides the life class. Industrialist and avid sports fan, Charles Wheeler, commissioned Gaudier to 'make two little statues in plaster' in 1912. One was to be of a wrestler and the other of a bather. No extant copy of the bather survives, or perhaps it was never made, but Gaudier did execute the wrestler (*The Wrestler*, 1912–13, fig. 22).[9] In preparation, he

najdrozejsza — Je suis très fatigué car je n'ai fait
que courir d'un côté sur l'autre et ai beaucoup
travaillé cette semaine. Hier soir je suis allé
voir les lutteurs. ma foi je n'ai jamais vu
d'aussi beau spectacle. 2 athlètes typiques —
larges épaules, trapus, énorme cou de bœuf,
petite taille, cuisses fermes, chevilles fines,
pieds prenants comme des mains, et pas hauts
mais ils se battent avec une vivacité un
entrain fabuleux, tournent en l'air, retombent
sur la tête pour être debout de l'autre côté
absolument incompréhensible. — Ils en sont
arrivé à cela, un a pu attraper l'autre
par les pieds et sans exagération l'a fait
tourner vertigineusement 5 fois autour de
soi puis l'a lâché, l'autre parti comme
une balle est tombé sur la tête, fait un
soubresaut et revint plus féroce à la batte.
On croyait qu'il allait se relever en p'tits
bouts. —

J'y suis resté 2 heures ai dessiné et vais
commencer les statuettes ce dimanche. —
Les négociations pour l'atelier à £ 30 n'ont
pas abouties, j'en cherche un autre.

reported to Sophie that he was 'going to see wrestling in the evenings two or three times, which will give me some good sketches; I am also going to see some boxing matches and diving, and I'm terribly excited about it'.[10] In the London Wrestling Club, just off Fleet Street, Gaudier revelled in watching the action going on around him and there are a number of sketches that might be associated with these visits, including the small and rapid pencil sketches of athletes (pl. 23). Gaudier was animated by what he saw and it was not so much the violence of the fight that enthralled him, but the energy of the encounter and dynamism of the wrestlers' movements. He described the 'amazing vivacity and spirit' of the wrestlers he watched in the homosocial world of the wrestling club as they moved (fig. 20):

'... turning in the air, falling back on their heads, and in a flash were up again on the other side, utterly incomprehensible. They have reached such a state of perfection that one can take the other by a foot and, without exaggeration, can whirl him five times round and round himself, and then let go so that the other flies off like a ball and falls on his head – but he is up in a moment and back again more ferocious than ever to the fight. [I] thought he would be smashed to bits. I stayed and drew for two hours and am going to begin the statuettes on Sunday.'[11]

As is so powerfully suggested by this exhibition, Gaudier's interest in the fighting form should be viewed in the context of his much broader study of the athletic body and the body in movement.[12] Gaudier's interest in the rhythmic movement of the athletically trained body can be detected across his studies of dancers and wrestlers, and his depictions of wrestlers were never solely about the sport of wrestling *per se*.[13] In his pencil drawing *Two Wrestlers* (1913, pl. 43) (which is very close to the artist's Omega Workshops marquetry tray design), Gaudier appears to bring dancing and wrestling together. The large, bulky forms of the fighters dance around one another, with heads cocked, limbs raised forwards and back arms thrown up and out to the side whilst the hands closest to each other come together to swing each partner round. Without the title, we might be forgiven for thinking that this is the scene of some ritualistic folk dance rather than a moment of combat paused by Gaudier's pencil.

As well as the rhythmic potential of the fight or grapple, Gaudier also seems to have delighted in its ambiguities. Friends or foe? Fierce or fun? Combat or carouse? Grapple or jig? Looking at the series of works concerning wrestling that Gaudier executed in a short but intense period of activity between 1912 and 1914 it is often difficult to tell. This is especially the case in the works depicting wrestling associated with the Omega Workshops, such as the aforementioned wooden tray with marquetry (pl. 44), which bares striking similarities to the cubed and angular depictions of the fighters' forms employed by David Bomberg in his painting *Ju-Jitsu* (c. 1913, oil on board, Tate). The decorative potential of the interlocking forms of the interlacing bodies is emphasized to great effect in Gaudier's linocut of *The Wrestlers* (pl. 48), designed to be used as a Christmas card.[14] This is also the case with the plaster *Wrestlers relief* where the smooth, almost elastic forms of the fighters seem to wrap around one another in embrace as opposed to aggression (is it too fanciful even to suggest that the wrestler on the topside of the hold is smiling?).[15] Gaudier's designs also frequently alluded to the potential erotics of the wrestling grapple, at once violent and intimate, and many of these works of wrestlers and wrestling fall somewhere between combat and the comedic, or strength and sensuality (pl. 49). And as well as dynamic movement there are also moments of stillness in Gaudier's scenes of combat, for example in the lock of the hold of the figures on the relief, of the pregnant pause, eyeing one another up, the face-off before the grapple begins (fig. 21), or the moment of defeat in the drawing in which one wrestler's head is pinned to the ground (pl. 47).

fig. 21
Henri Gaudier-Brzeska
Wrestlers, c. 1913, pencil
on paper, 260 × 380 mm
The Sherwin Collection, Leeds

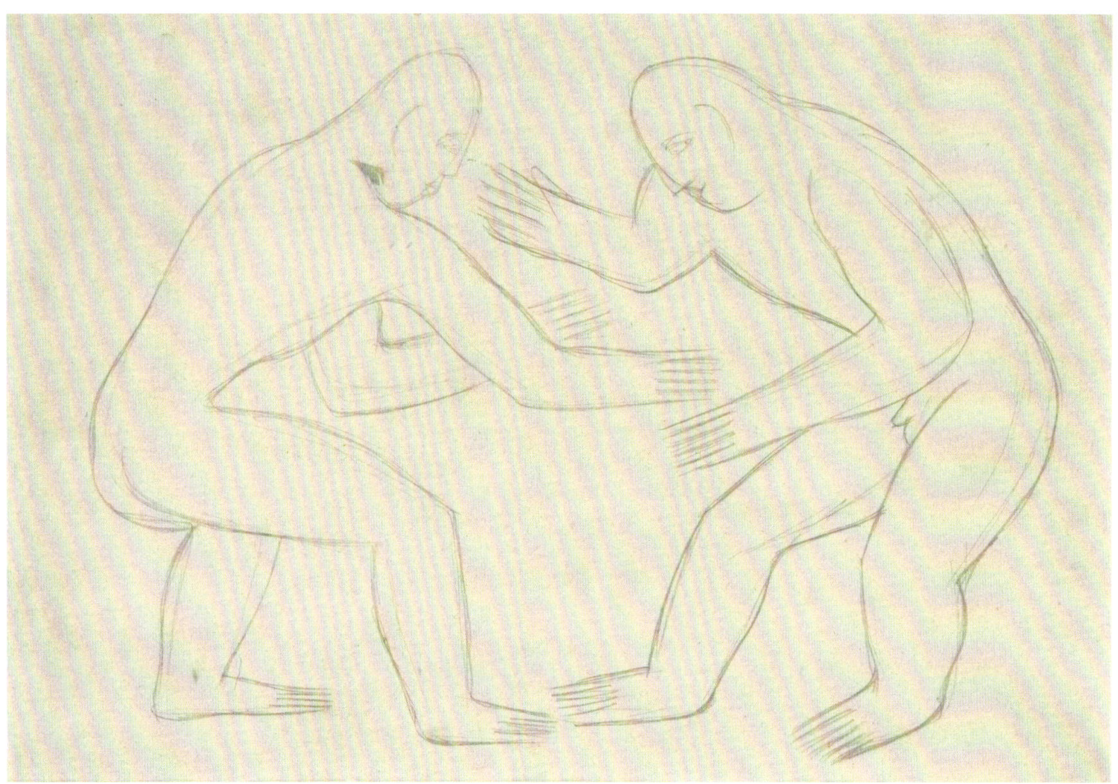

There are at least ten known drawings associated with the
subject of wrestling, plus two sculptures, one wooden tray and
a linocut, all made by Gaudier in an intense burst of activity
between 1912 and 1914.[16] Judging from Gaudier's levels of
productivity, there were probably many more associated
drawings that are now lost. Undoubtedly, it was a topic of some
fascination to him, but to see wrestling simply as subject matter
does not quite get to the heart of its allure for Gaudier. Writing
about the literary avant-garde's fascination with boxing and
pugilism, the cultural historian Kasia Boddy suggests that these
sports were not only used as a subject but 'the basis for a
method'.[17] At the same time that Gaudier was depicting
wrestling and violence, he was also writing in his letters and
contemporary journals and magazines about modern sculpture
using a language of force, strength and power, and eagerly
cultivating a tough, combative and virile artistic persona. By
employing a credo of violence and force Gaudier, along with a
number of his contemporaries associated with the Vorticist and
Futurist movements, embodied a concept of the avant-garde
artist that was in opposition to the well-dressed, art school
trained aesthete, widely caricatured in the late-Victorian and
Edwardian periods. The 'modern sculptor', he wrote is 'a man
who works with instinct as his inspiring force […] The shape
of a leg, or the curve of an eyebrow, etc. etc., have to him no
significance whatsoever; light voluptuous modelling is to him
insipid – what he feels he does so intensely'.[18] Gaudier also
saw sculpture as a form of physical training, pummelling clay,
sketching rapidly across the page, knocking off lumps of plaster
and stone – there was a force and intensity to his untrained
technique. He identified with the athletic speed and vigour of
the wrestlers he saw in the gymnasium – strong, small and
quick like himself – but he also saw in the subject of wrestling
a way to bring together stillness and movement, rhythm and
strength, aesthetics and violence. In these drawings, designs
and sculptures of wrestlers, Gaudier's ultimate goal seems to
have been to test out the body, often pushing it to it very limits,
and even beyond.

fig. 22
Henri Gaudier-Brzeska,
The Wrestler, 1912 – 13,
bronze cast 1945, 635 × 270 × 450 mm,
K5164, Bristol Museum and Art Gallery

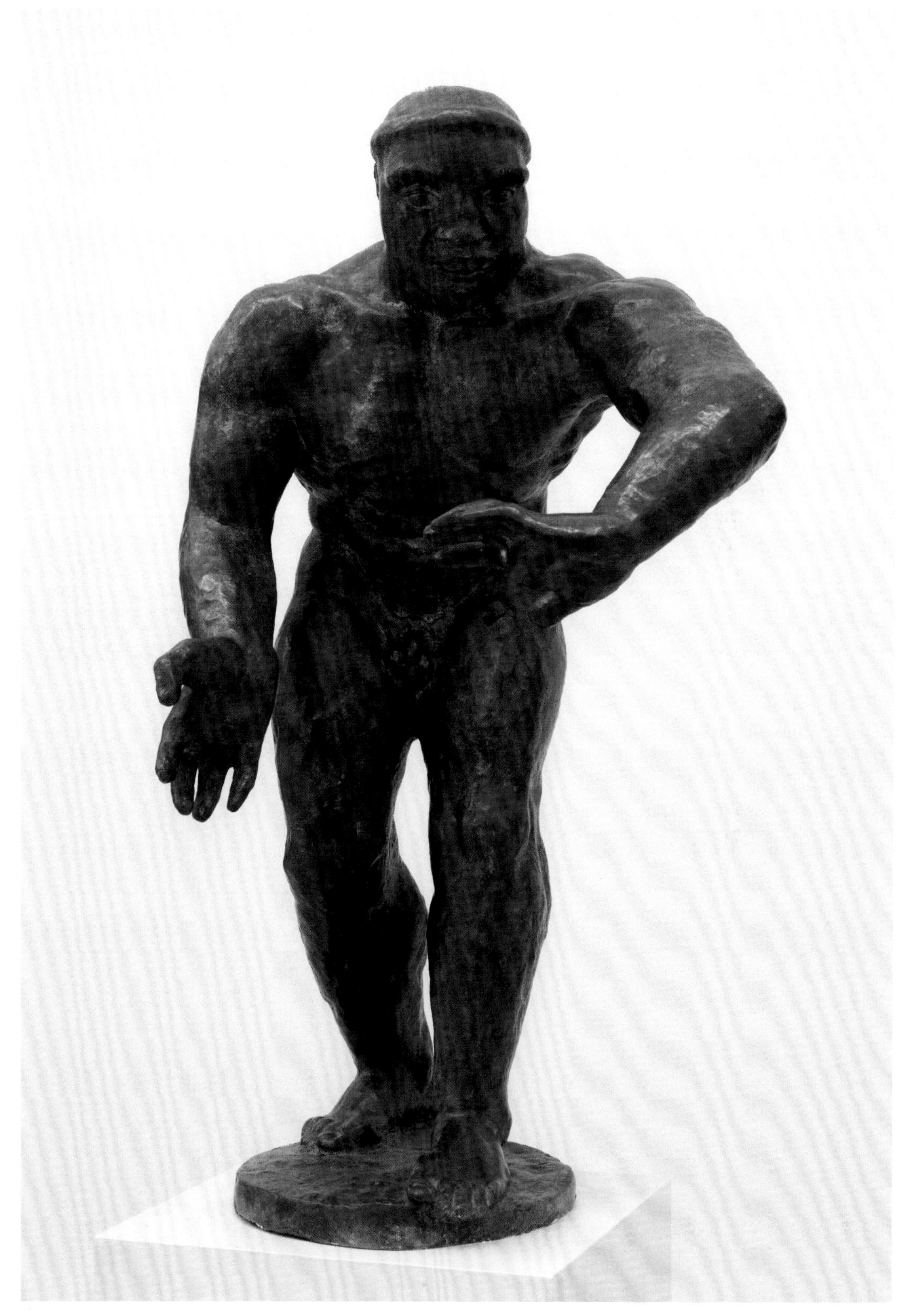

1
D. H. Lawrence, *Women in Love*, New York, 1995 (first published 1920), p. 270.

2
For a much extended discussion of Gaudier's *Wrestlers* relief, see my 'In Focus' essay on this art work in Tate collection, http://www.tate.org.uk/art/research-publications/gaudier-brzeska-wrestlers. I thank Jennifer Mundy and Christopher Griffin for encouraging me to develop my work on Gaudier's *Wrestlers relief*, from which this essay stems. Comments in response to papers on Gaudier and wrestling at the Henry Moore Institute, Leeds, and Trinity College, Dublin, have been tremendously helpful in developing the ideas presented here.

3
Bernard Vere, '"BLAST SPORT"? Vorticism, Sport, and William Roberts's *Boxers*', unpublished paper. I would like to thank Bernard Vere for sharing this work with me. Jon Wood and Mark Antliff's research on Gaudier has also been influencial for my interpretation of this sculpture. I thank them for their insights and discussions on this subject.

4
See Neil Carter, 'British Boxing's Colour Bar, 1911–48', Black History Season, The Hidden History of Black British Sport, DMU, 22 November 2011, available at https://www.academia.edu/3190661/British_Boxing_s_Colour_Bar_1911–48. The colour bar was repealed in 1948. Many thanks to Bernard Vere for suggesting this possible connection.

5
Anon., 'Boxing: The Referee and his Duties', *Times*, 14 January 1911, p. 15.

6
Rupert R. Arrowsmith, *Modernism and the Museum; Asian, African and Pacific Art and the London Avant-Garde*, Oxford, 2011.

7
Gaudier, in H. S. Ede, *Savage Messiah*, Heinemann, London, 1931, pp. 209–10.

8
A connected drawing is housed in Tate's collection – *Wrestler*, 1913, ink on paper, 384 × 251 mm, presented by Kettle's Yard Collection, Cambridge 1966, T00850.

9
According to the art historian Paul O'Keeffe, Wheeler did not purchase *Wrestler*. Wheeler, O'Keeffe notes, probably intended the statues to be sporting trophies and 'therefore needed to be no more than six or nine inches high, a fraction of the size Gaudier-Brzeska had produced'. Paul O'Keeffe, *Henri Gaudier-Brzeska: An Absolute Case of Genius*, London, 2004, p. 165.

10
Ede, 1931, p. 210.

11
Gaudier to Sophie Brzeska, letter, 3 December 1912, quoted in Ede, 1931, pp. 218.

12
For more on Gaudier's interest in movement and the body, see Evelyn Silber's essay in this catalogue and also her book *Gaudier-Brzeska: Life and Art*, London, 1996, p. 102.

13
His contemporary, William Roberts, also shared this dual interest in depicting fighting and dancing, as did fellow Omega artist, Duncan Grant. I thank Hana Leaper for pointing out this overlap of subject matter with Grant and for her comments on this essay.

14
'Brzeska saw me at work, cutting designs at my home, and he decided to do some also. Being near Christmas time he cut a version of his *Wrestlers*, to be used as a card. [This] is his only effort at cutting. It was printed on my etching-press.' Horace Brodzky, *Henri Gaudier-Brzeska, 1891–1915*, London, 1933, p. 44–5.

15
According to H. S. Ede the work was once mis-catalogued as the 'Lovers'. See Lewison's catalogue entry on the work 1983, cat. 78, p. 55.

16
Francine A. Koslow, 'The Evolution of Henri Gaudier-Brzeska's "Wrestlers" Relief', *Museum Bulletin of the Museum of Fine Arts Boston*, vol. 78, 1980, p. 42.

17
Kasia Boddy, *Boxing: A Cultural History*, London, 2008, p. 58.

18
Gaudier, draft letter to *The Egoist*, 1914, Tate Archive, TGA 91133.

41
Male Nude, c. 1912 – 13

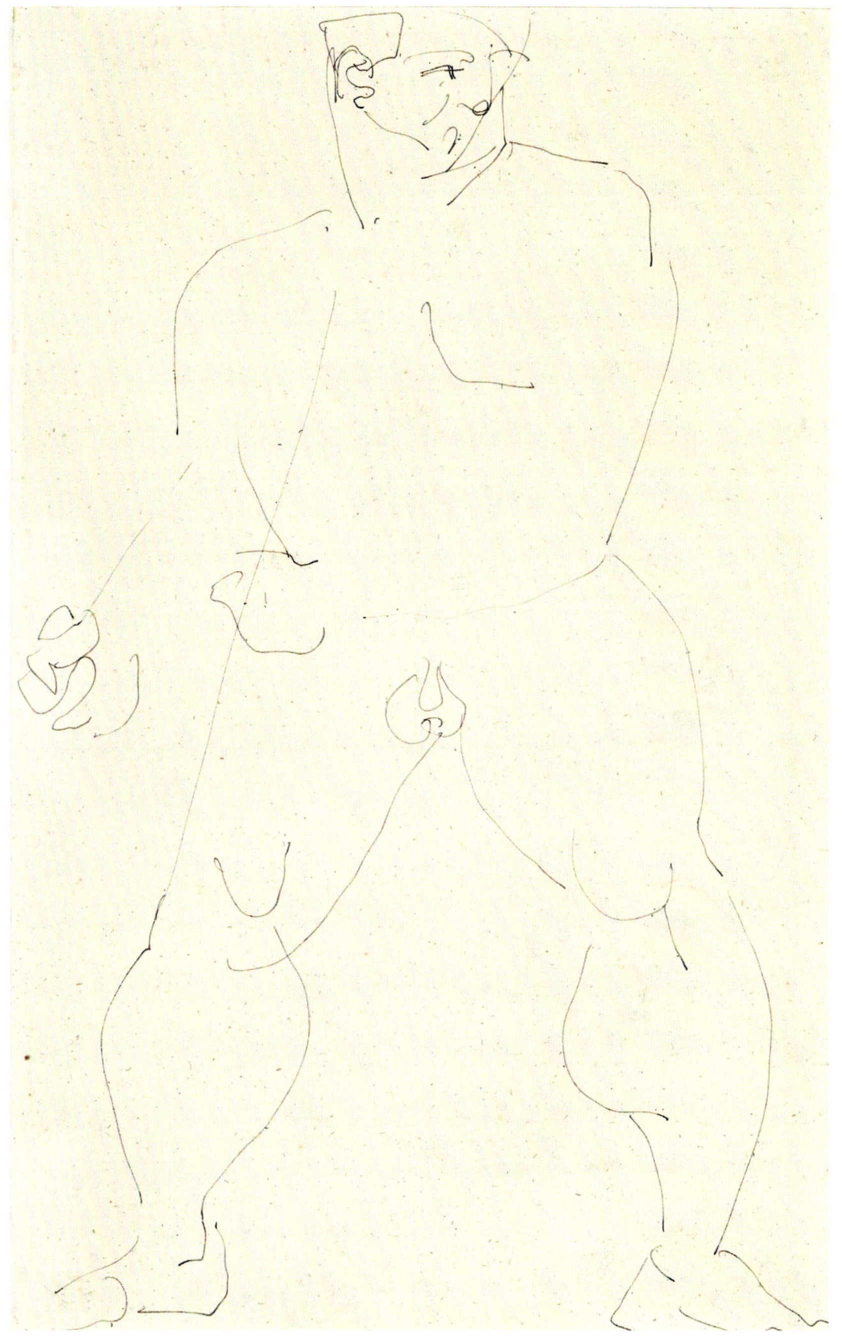

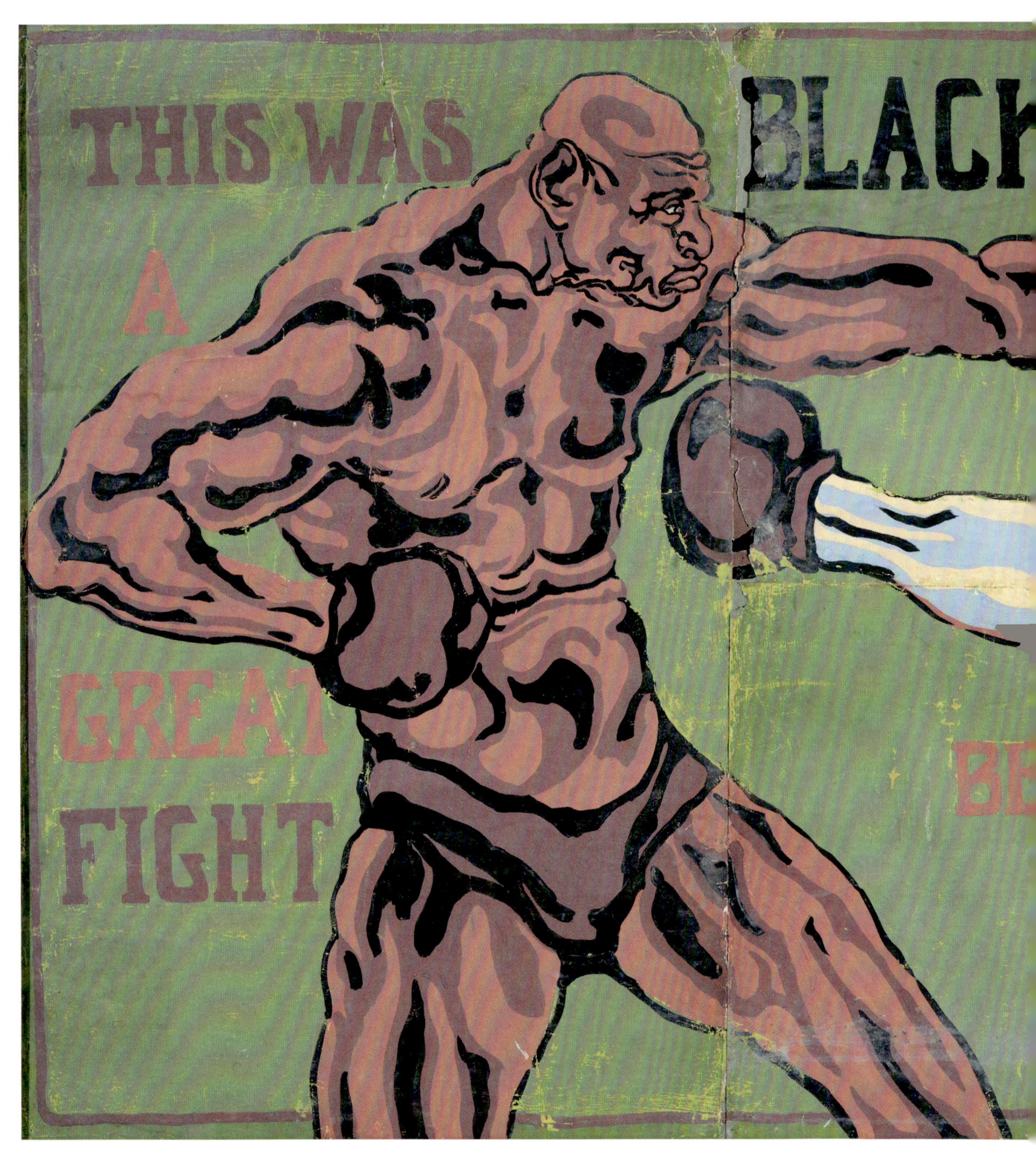

42
*Black & White poster
(aka Boxers)*, 1911

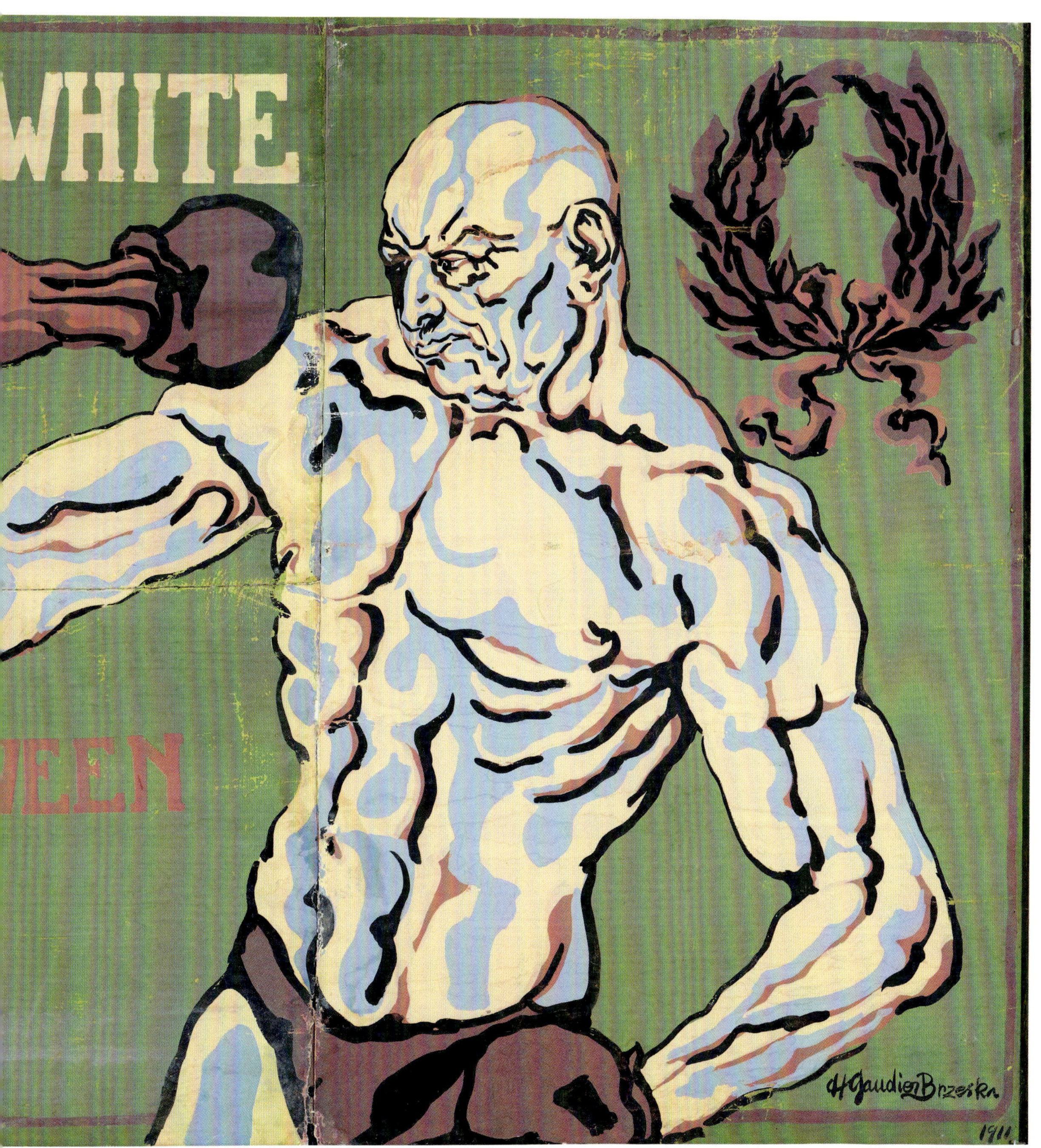
WHITE
EEN
H Gaudier Brzeska
1911

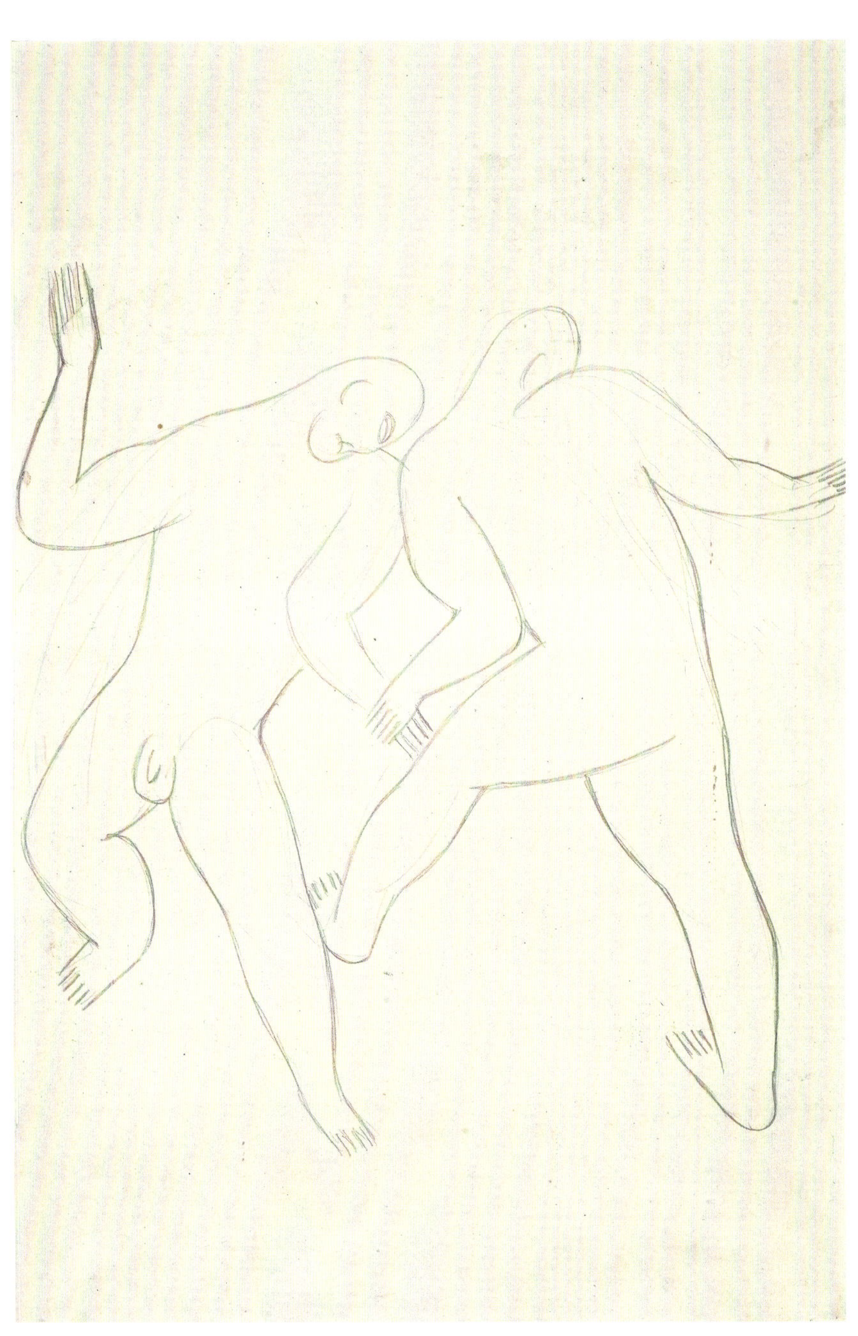

43
Two Wrestlers, c. 1913

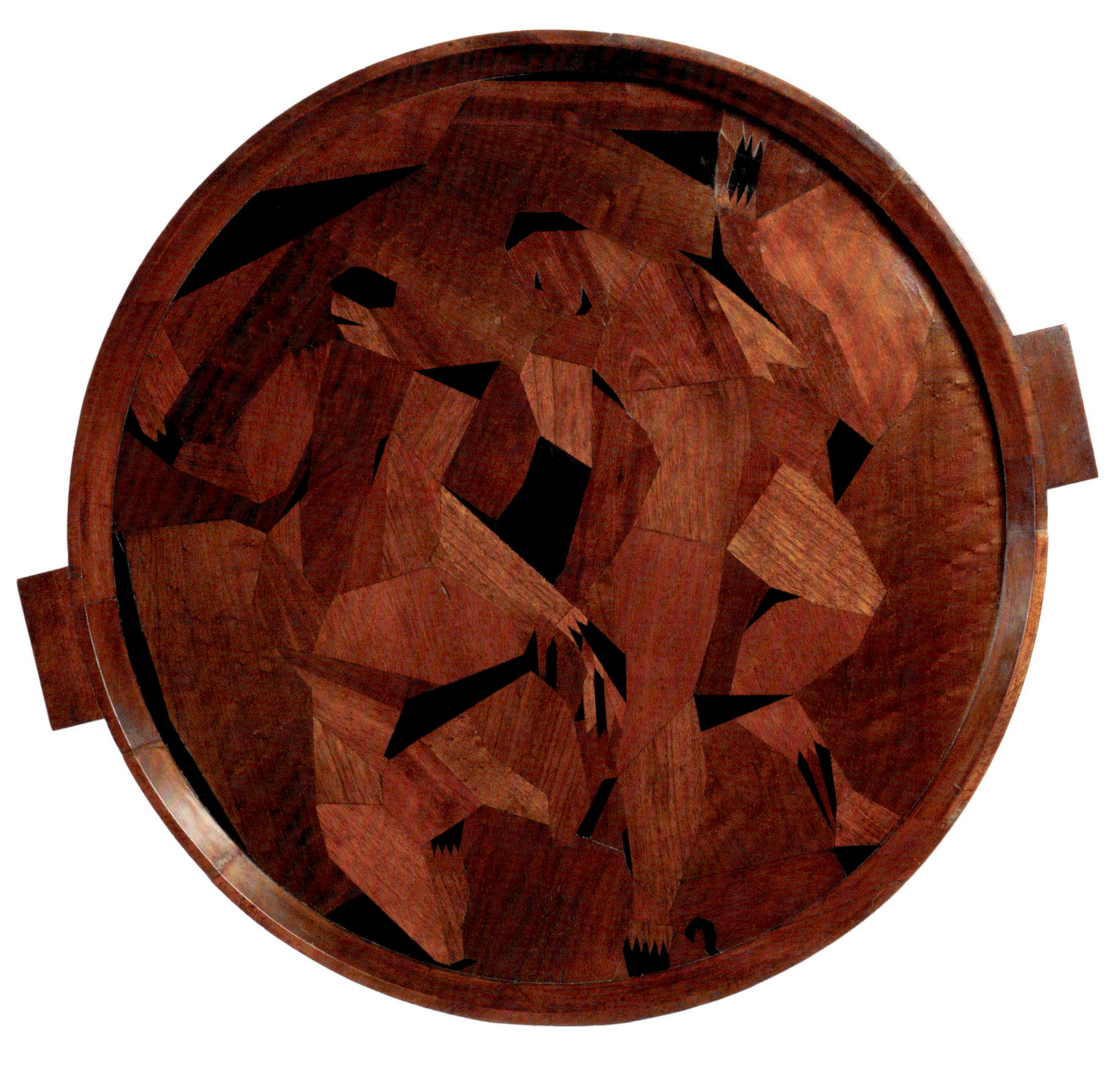

44
The Wrestlers tray, 1913

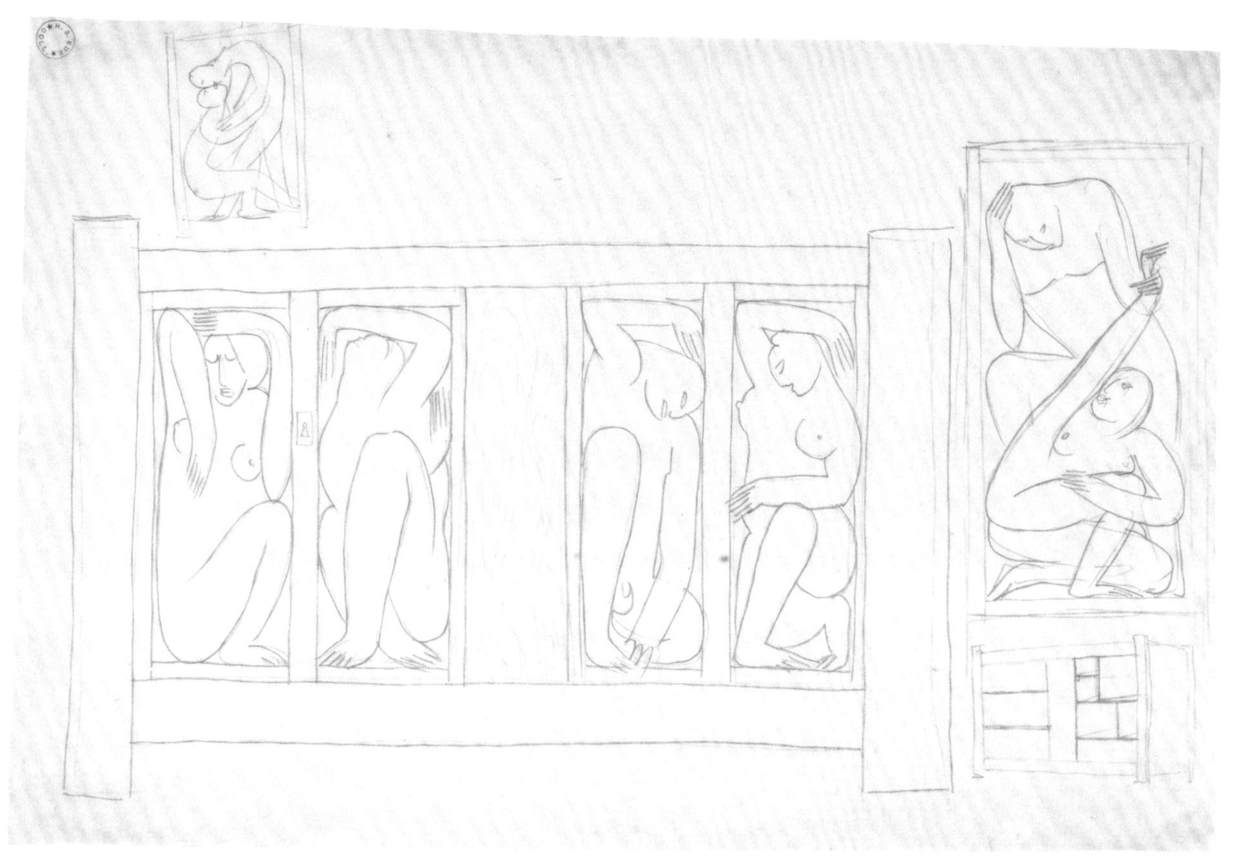

45
Design for furniture for Roger Fry's
Omega Workshops, 1913

46
Two Men Wrestling, c. 1913

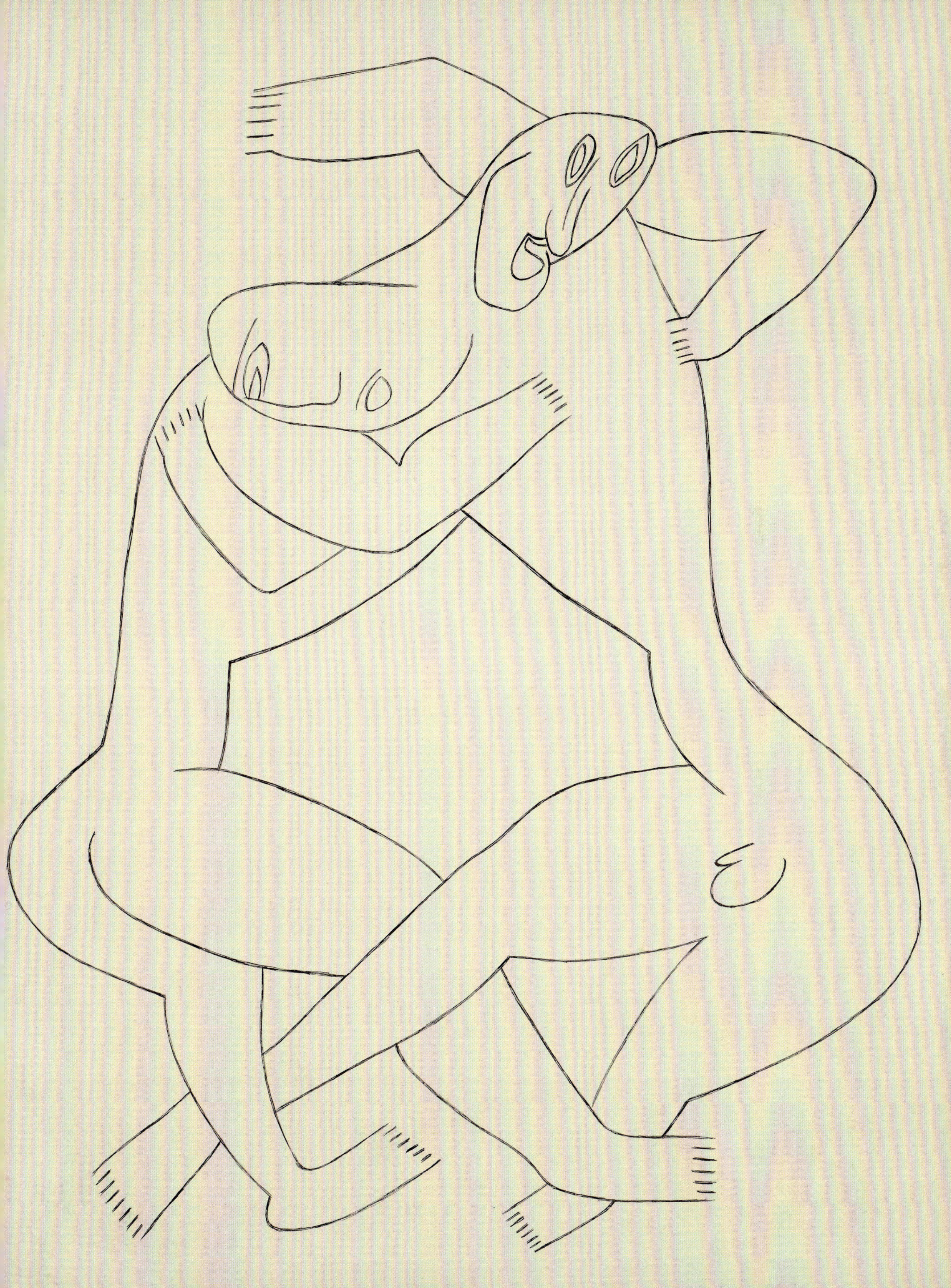

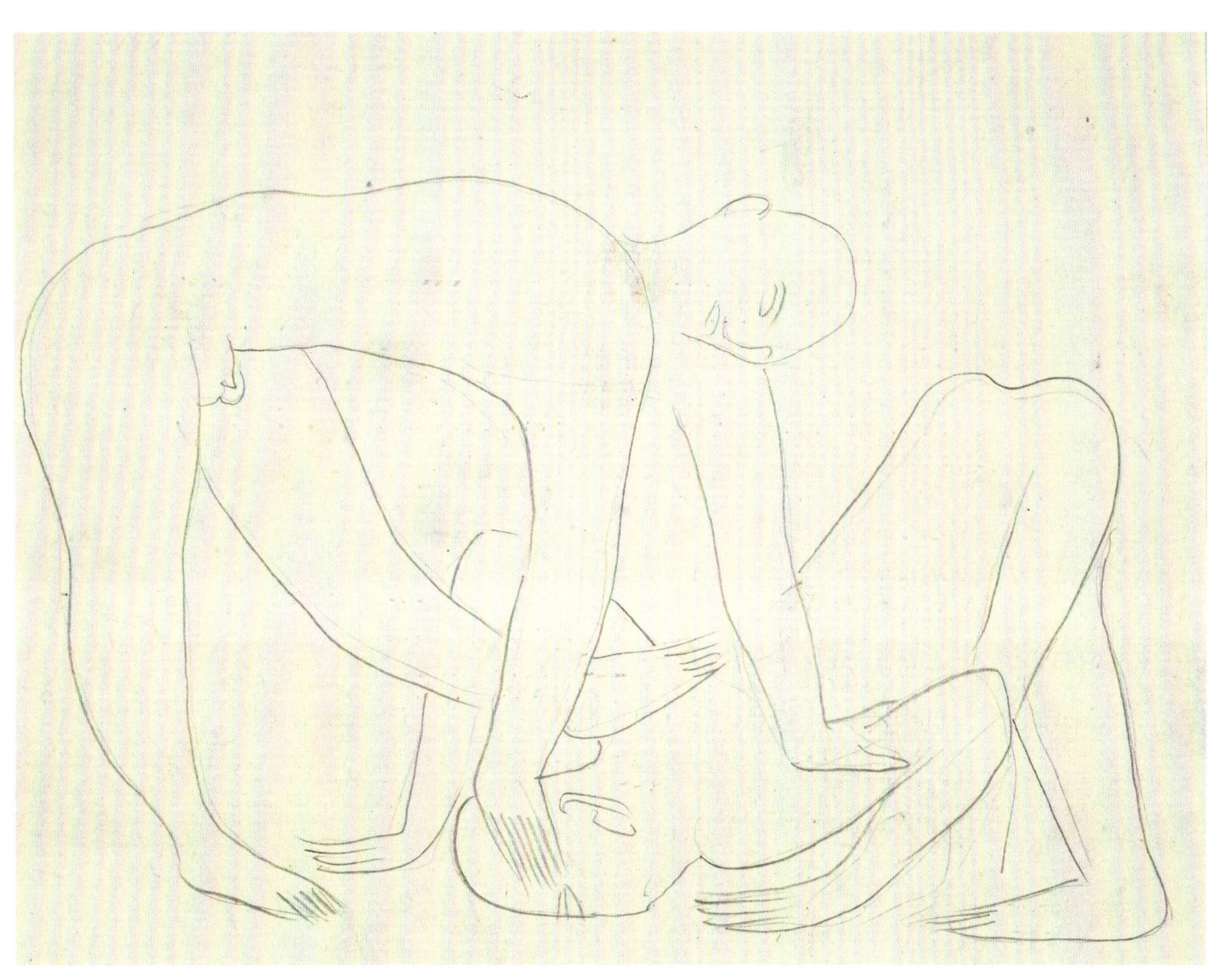

47
Two Wrestlers, 1914

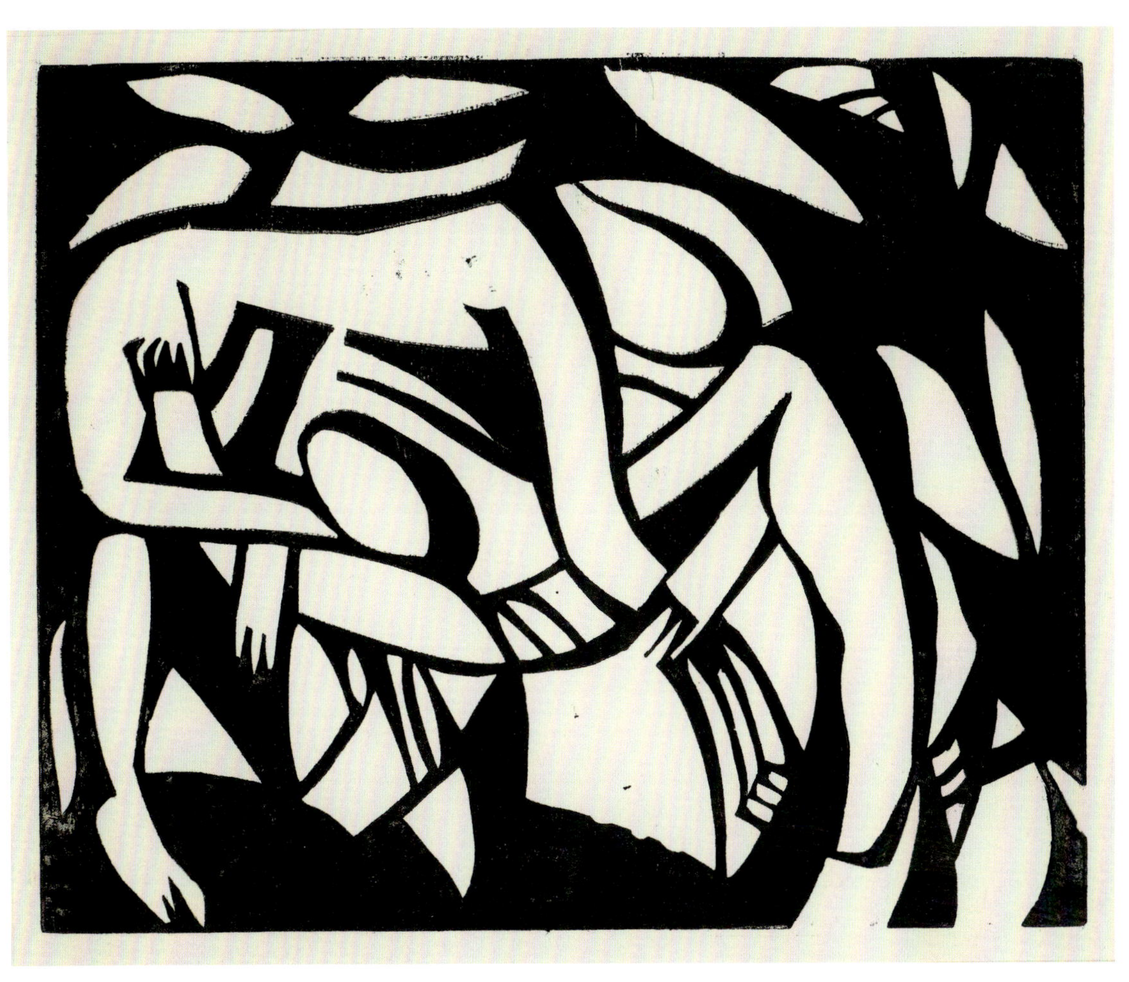

48
Wrestlers, 1914

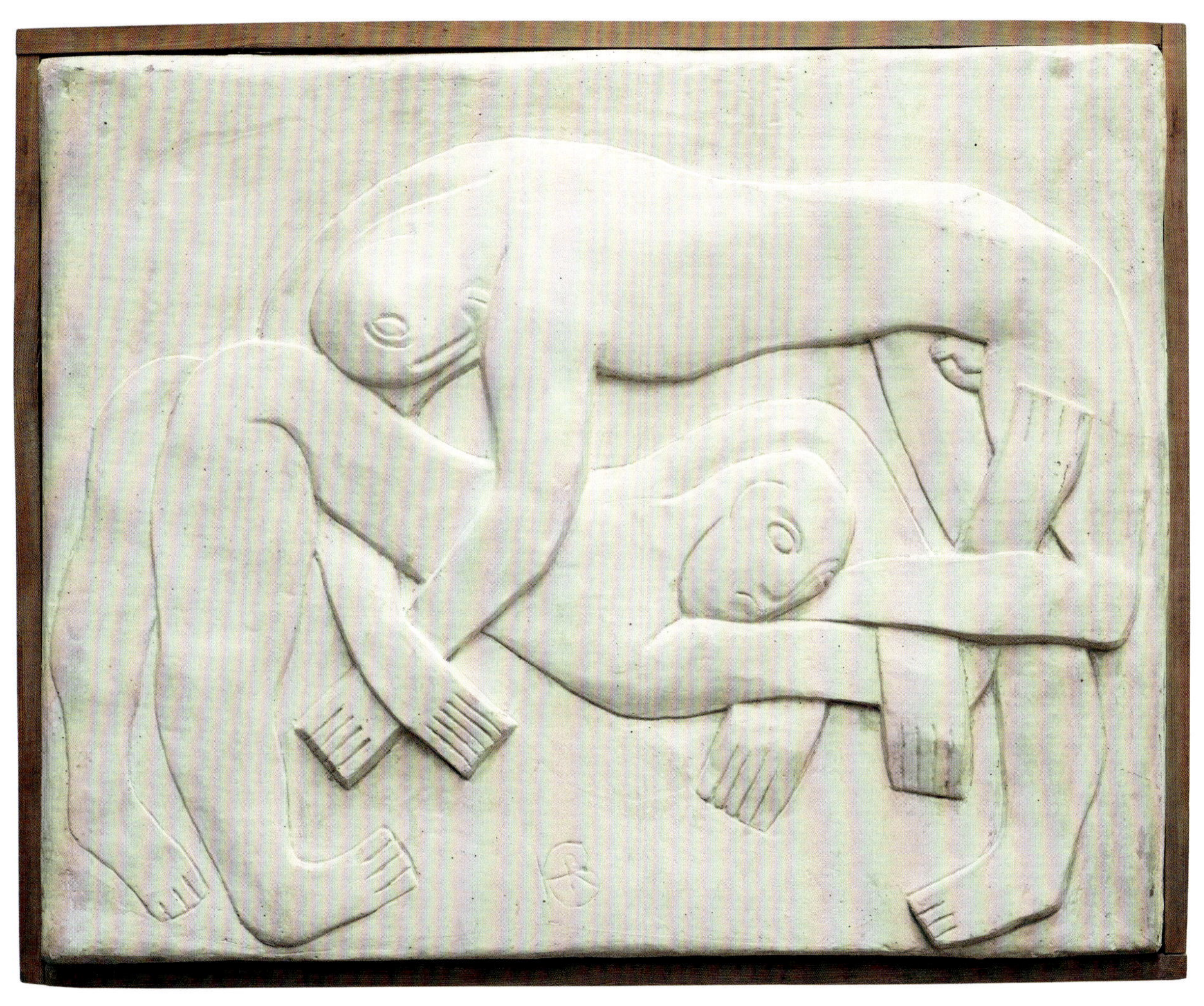

49
Wrestlers relief, c. 1913–14,
herculite cast 1965

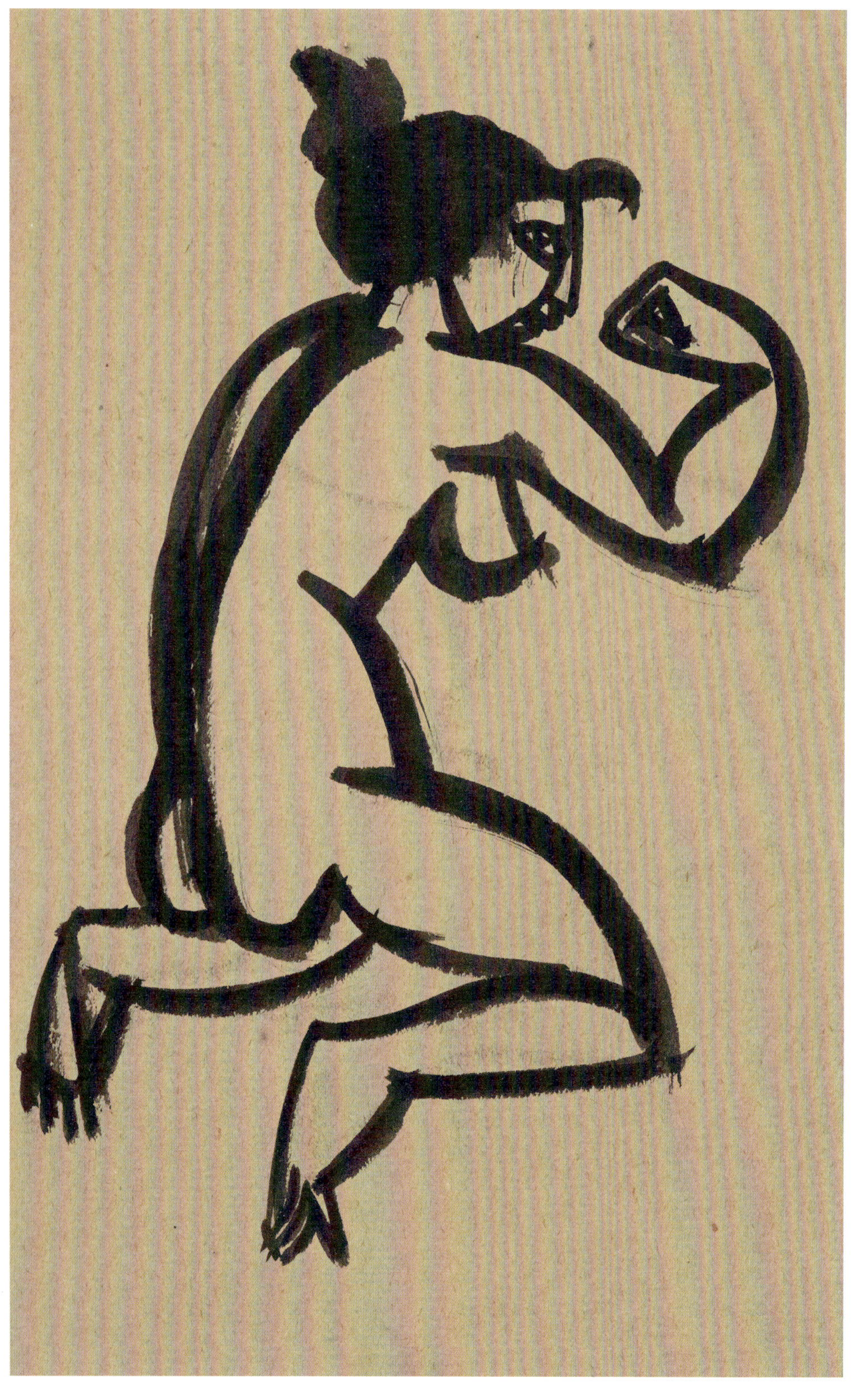

51
Seated figure c. 1912 – 13

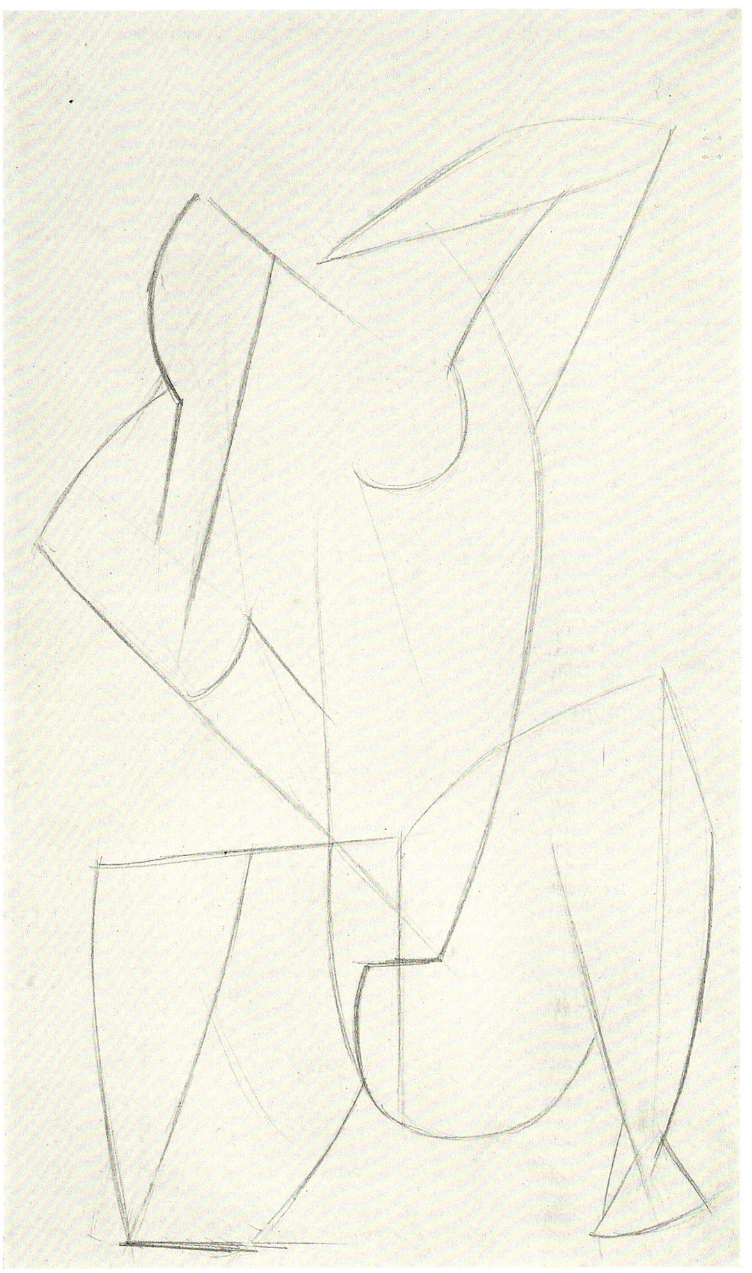

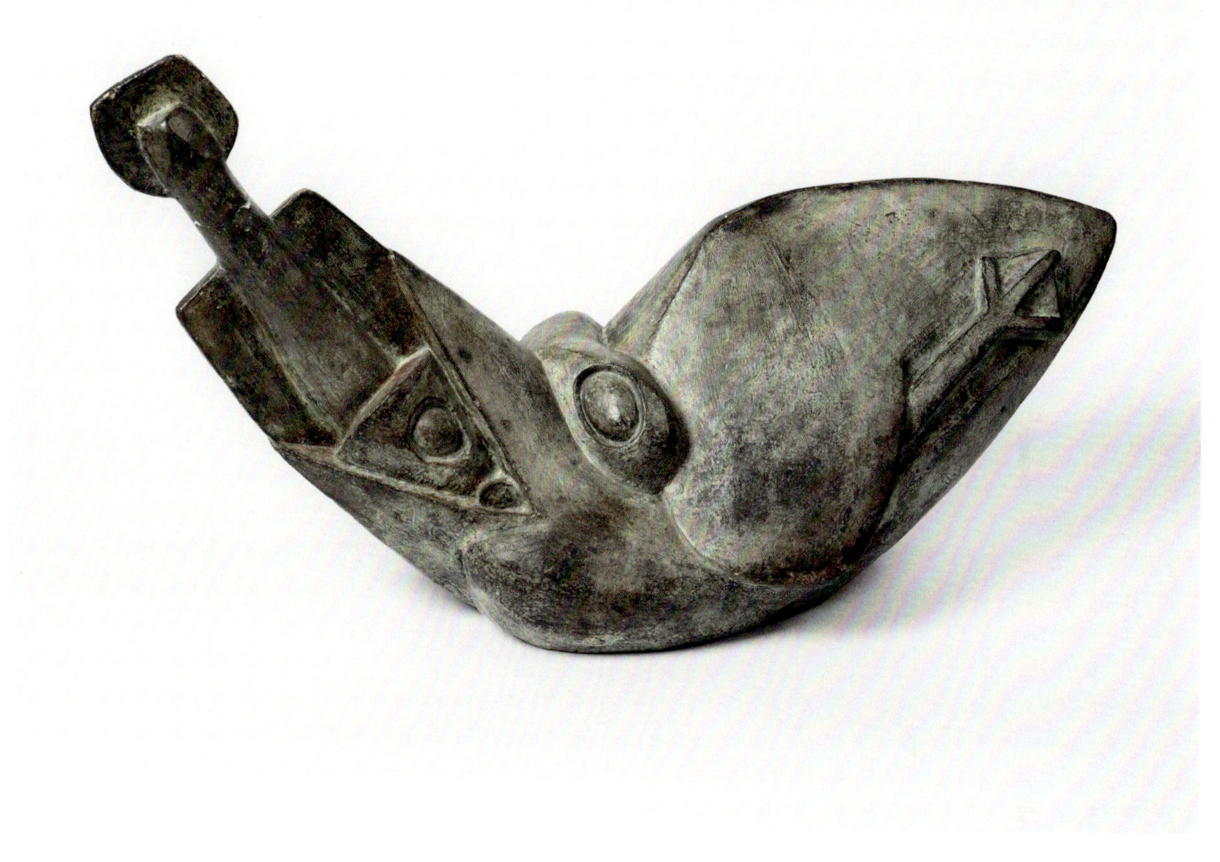

52
Bird Swallowing a Fish, 1914

Chronology

1891

Henri Gaudier is born on 4 October, Saint Jean de Braye, near Orléans, France. He is educated in Saint Jean de Braye and Orléans.

1906 –08

Gaudier wins prizes to travel first to London (June – July 1906), then a two-year scholarship to study abroad, which he begins in Bristol (September 1907). He studies business and visits Bath, Somerset and Wales. Gaudier then moves to Cardiff (September/October 1908) to work in the offices of coal importers Fitfoot and Ching.

He sketches in the open-air and in museums during these trips.

1909

After a brief stop in London, where he sketches at the British Museum, Gaudier travels to Nuremberg for further business study. He meets Dr. Uhlemayr in April, who provides continued support. He also travels to Munich. Gaudier learns to speak German during these trips and sketches. He returns to Paris in September and lives in Montparnasse.

1910

Works as a clerk and translator, but sketches in the evenings at the Bibliothèque Sainte-Geneviève where he meets 38 year-old Zofia (Sophie) Brzeska who becomes his partner.

Between May and June, Gaudier decides to devote himself to art and to sculpture.

He returns to Orléans for a short time with Sophie.

Exhibitions and
Popular Culture

1907

French philosopher Henri Bergson's *L'Évolution créatrice* is published which Gaudier reads. The book is translated into English in 1911.

1909

The Ballets Russes is founded by Serge Diaghilev. Its first season opens at the Théâtre Châtelet, Paris.

Fillipo Tommaso Marinetti publishes his First Futurist Manifesto in *Figaro*, 20 February.

1910

The Ballets Russes premiere *L'Oiseau de Feu* (The Firebird) in Paris on the 25 June.

Roger Fry organises the exhibition *Manet and the Post-Impressionists* at the Grafton Galleries, London.

1911
Henri Gaudier-Brzeska

Gaudier moves to London with Sophie in January and adds her surname to his own; he henceforth becomes known as Henri Gaudier-Brzeska.

He lives in Hammersmith, Shepherd's Bush and then Chelsea and works as a clerk and translator, employed by a Norwegian shipping company.

He sketches regularly in markets, at London Zoo and in the British Museum and produces a number of poster designs including one for Black & White Whisky.

Exhibitions and Popular Culture

Paul Gsell's book *L'Art* is published in Paris containing contemporary interviews with French sculptor Auguste Rodin. It is translated in to English in 1912.

The first issue of *Rhythm* magazine is published in the summer by John Middleton Murry. John Duncan Fergusson is arts editor.

Diaghilev's Ballets Russes performs its second season in Paris. They also premiere in London.

1912
Henri Gaudier-Brzeska

Gaudier meets patrons including Haldane Macfall, Major Smythies, Lovat Fraser, Thomas Leman Hare and meets the novelist Enid Bagnold. He works on numerous portrait busts.

He moves to another studio in Chelsea (12 Redburn Street).

In June, Gaudier visits London Zoo and makes numerous sketches of animals from life.

Gaudier meets Murry, the editor of *Rhythm* magazine, and his wife Katherine Mansfield. He also visits Jacob Epstein's studio for the first time on 12 June and again in November.

In November, Gaudier attends life drawings classes and also reads Paul Gsell's *L'Art*.

He visits the London Wrestling Club in December, which inspires numerous drawings and sculptures.

Exhibitions and Popular Culture

The Miracle, a play by Max Reinhardt opens at The Olympia, London, in January. Gaudier attends and receives his first commission for a sculpture.

In March, the *Exhibition of Works by Italian Futurist Painters* opens at the Sackville Gallery, London.

The Ballets Russes perform *L'Oiseau de Feu* (The Firebird) to music by
Igor Stravinsky in London (12 June – 1 August). Gaudier is commissioned
to make a sculpture inspired by the ballet.

Mme Frida Strindberg opens the cabaret club *The Cave of the Golden Calf*,
Heddon Street, London (it runs until early 1914). Artists Jacob Epstein,
Eric Gill, Spencer Gore and Percy Wyndham Lewis variously produce
designs for the interior, and marketing materials. Lewis' painting *Kermesse*
is hung in the club.

Gaudier's drawings are published in two issues of *Rhythm* magazine in
September and October.

J. E. Crawford Flitch's book *Modern Dancing and Dancers* is published.

1913
Henri Gaudier-Brzeska

Gaudier moves to three new London studios – two in Fulham and
one in Putney (25 Winthorpe Road).

He meets the artist and writer Horace Brodzky in January.

In July, Gaudier gives up his job as a clerk and devotes himself entirely
to the pursuit of art. He joins Roger Fry's Omega Workshops in the
autumn/winter.

Gaudier meets the poet and writer Ezra Pound, French sculptor
Constantin Brancusi and artist Nina Hamnett, at the Allied Artists'
Exhibition. In the summer and autumn he draws Hamnett and
models busts and figures.

He models *The Dancer* in clay and begins carving *Red Stone Dancer* later
in the year.

Exhibitions and Popular Culture

In April, Roger Fry announces the foundation of his Omega Workshops
in *Art Chronicle;* it opens in July at 33 Fitzroy Square (running until 1919).

In July, Fry includes Omega Workshops' artists' works in the *Ideal Home
Exhibition*, Olympia, London.

Brancusi visits Epstein's studio and the British Museum.
The Ballets Russes premiere *Le Sacre du Printemps* (The Rite of Spring)
on 29 May at the Théâtre des Champs-Élysées. It is premiered in London
at the Theatre Royal, Drury Lane, on 25 June.

Gaudier exhibits six works including *The Firebird* at the Allied
Artists' Association exhibition, Albert Hall, London. It is his first
public exhibition.

Lewis, Frederic Etchells, and Edward Wadsworth terminate association with Fry's Omega Workshops on 5 October. They form a 'Rebel Group' and invite Christopher R. W. Nevinson to join.

Alexander Archipenko's *The Dance* is reproduced on the cover of *The Sketch* magazine on 29 October.

Epstein's first solo show is held at the Adelphi Gallery, London, December.

The Apache Dancer, directed by Joseph Jay Bamberger, is filmed. The American film directed by D. W. Griffith, *The Mothering Heart* (featuring apache dance) is released.

Tango becomes a dance craze in London. *Hullo Tango!* is performed at the Hippodrome, London. *The Girl on Film* is performed at the Gaiety Theatre.

1914
Henri Gaudier-Brzeska

Gaudier carves his *Wrestlers relief* in plaster and his monumental head of Ezra Pound in stone.

He writes his first essay for magazine *BLAST* entitled 'Vortex. Gaudier-Brzeska'.

On 20 September, Gaudier enrolls in the 129e Régiment d'Infanterie and leaves England to serve in WW1. He writes from the trenches to friends and supporters including Sophie, Ezra Pound and Edward Wadsworth. He continues to make sculpture and sketches and, in December, begins to write his second essay 'Vortex. Gaudier-Brzeska. (Written from the Trenches)' for *BLAST war number*.

Exhibitions and Popular Culture

In January, Gaudier exhibits five sculptures and drawings with the Grafton Group at the Alpine Gallery, including *Red Stone Dancer*.

Gaudier joins the London Group in February and participates in their exhibition at the Goupil Gallery, London. He exhibits five works including *Red Stone Dancer*.

Two sculptures and a drawing by Gaudier are reproduced in *The Egoist* magazine in March. Gaudier writes a review of the Allied Artists' exhibition for the magazine in June.

The New Age weekly magazine reproduces Gaudier's drawing of 'A Dancer' (19 March).

Wyndham Lewis opens his *Rebel Art Centre* in April (also known as
The Cubist Art Centre), offering an art school, workshop, venue for
performances and discussions. Gaudier is actively involved in the group.

The exhibition *Twentieth Century Art: A Review of Modern Movements* is held
at Whitechapel Art Gallery (8 May – 20 June). Gaudier exhibits six works
including *The Firebird*.

Marinetti and Nevinson publish 'The Vital English Art Futurist
Manifesto' in *The Observer* (1 June). Gaudier signs a letter with other
artists in response (14 June).

Gaudier exhibits at the Allied Artists' Association exhibition (June – July).

BLAST number 1 is published (15 June). It includes Gaudier's essay
'Vortex. Gaudier-Brzeska'.

In July, David Bomberg's first solo show is held at the Chenil Gallery, London.

John Rodker publishes *Poems by John Rodker* with a Bomberg dancer
sketch on the cover.

3 AUGUST 1914
GERMANY DECLARES WAR ON FRANCE

4 AUGUST 1914
BRITAIN DECLARES WAR ON GERMANY

1915
Henri Gaudier-Brzeska

Gaudier is promoted to Sergeant on 25 March.

HENRI GAUDIER-BRZESKA IS KILLED IN ACTION AT
NEUVILLE ST. VAAST, FRANCE ON 5 JUNE c. 3.30PM.

The artist's estate passes to Sophie Brzeska.

4 works by Gaudier are exhibited in the London Group Salon.

Exhibitions and
Visual Culture

The first *Vorticist Exhibition* is held at the Doré Galleries, London (10
June – July). It includes works by Jessica Dismorr, Frederick Etchells,
William Roberts, Helen Saunders, and Edward Wadsworth. Gaudier is
represented posthumously by eight sculptures including *Red Stone Dancer*.
William Roberts exhibits the (lost) painting *Twostep*.

In July, 'Vortex. Gaudier-Brzeska (Written from the Trenches)'
is published posthumously in *BLAST war number*.

1918

Ezra Pound organises *A Memorial Exhibition of the Work of Henri Gaudier*
is held at the Leicester Galleries. It includes *Red Stone Dancer* and
'The Russian Ballet' *(The Firebird). The Dancer* (bronze cast) and *Wrestlers
relief* are also exhibited for the first time. It is introduced by Ezra Pound.
Pound also publishes *Gaudier-Brzeska. A Memoir by Ezra Pound.* Gaudier,
Lewis, Roberts, Saunders and others are included in the *Vorticist
Exhibition*, Penguin Club, New York (July – August).

1919

The Ovid Press publishes 20 drawings from Gaudier's notebooks,
which includes a dancer sketch from the collection of Nina Hamnett.

1925

Sophie Brzeska dies in Gloucestershire on 17 March. On her death
Gaudier's estate and correspondence passes to the nation.

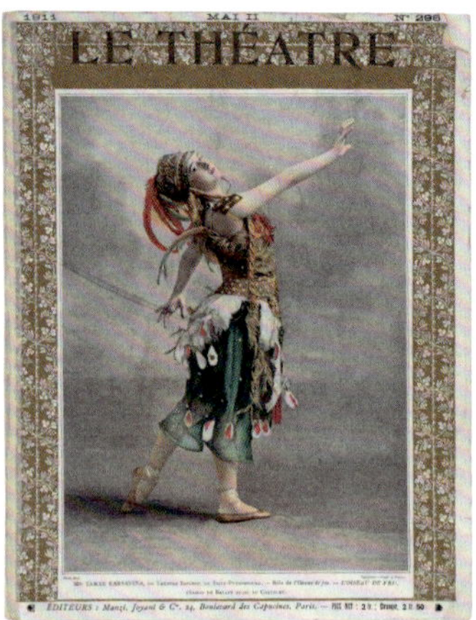

fig. 23

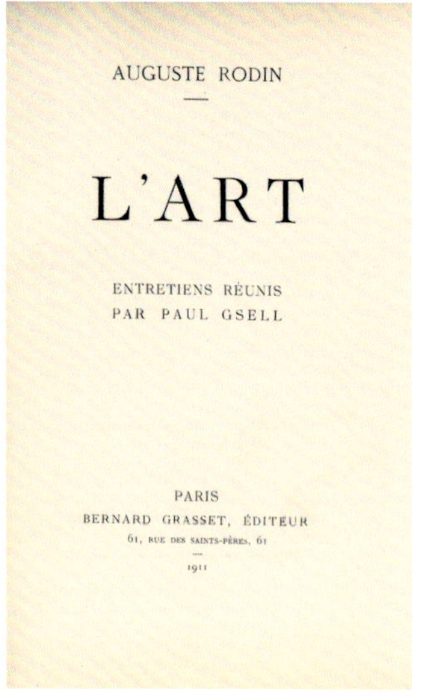

fig. 24

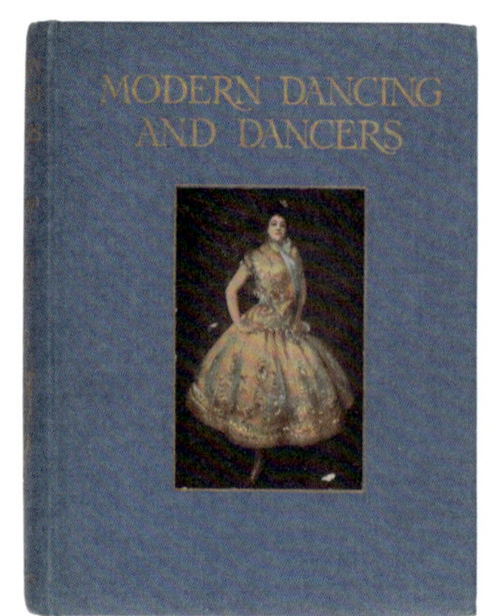

fig. 25

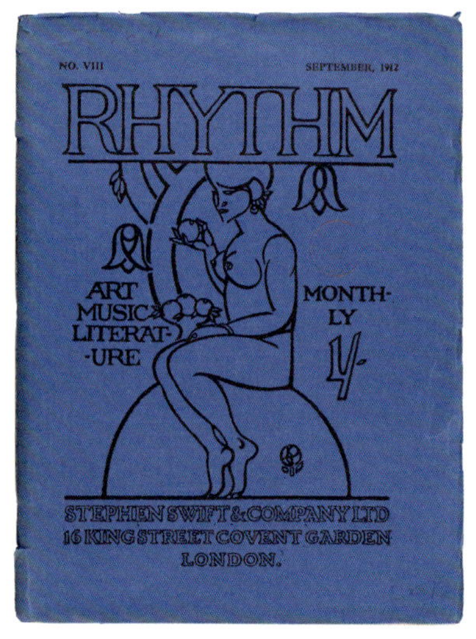

fig. 26

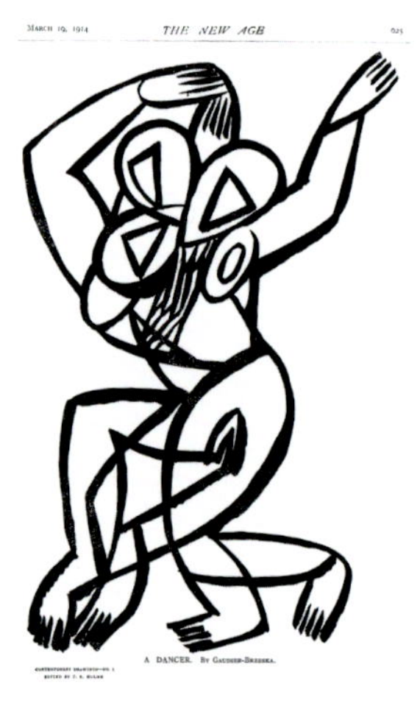

fig. 27

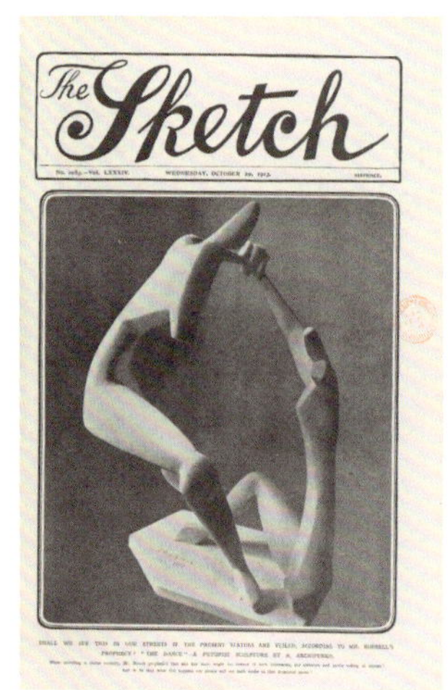

fig. 28

fig. 29

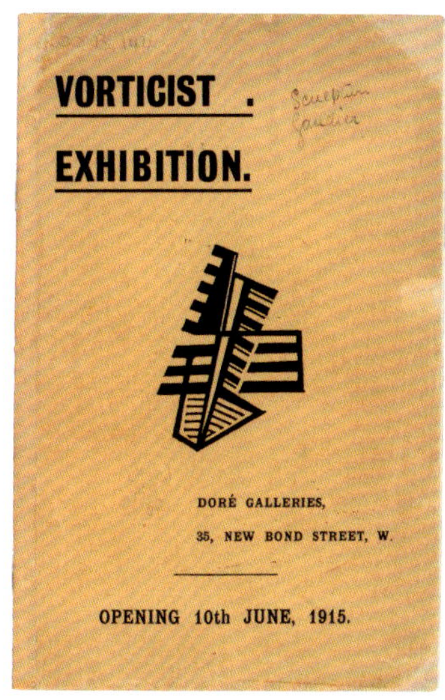

fig. 30

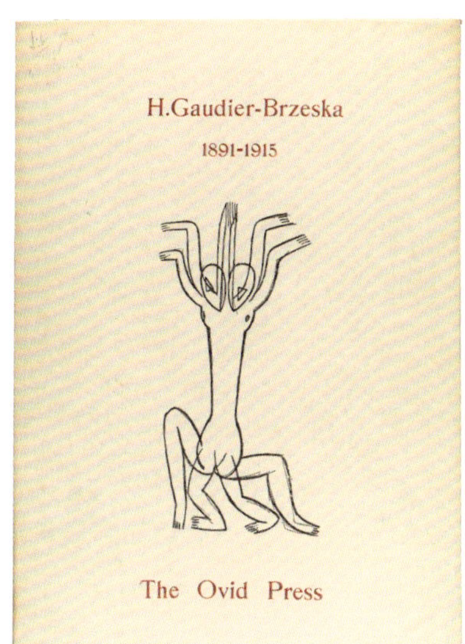

fig. 31

fig. 23
Le Théâtre, Paris, May 1911, cover showing Tamara
Karsavina as *L'Oiseau de feu* (The Firebird)

fig. 24
Paul Gsell, *L'Art*, Paris, 1911

fig. 25
J. E. Crawford Flitch, *Modern Dancing and Dancers,*
London, 1912, front cover

fig. 26
John Middleton Murry (ed.), *Rhythm: Art Music
Literature Monthly,* London, September 1912, vol. 2,
no. 8, containing drawings by Henri Gaudier-Brzeska,
Cambridge University Library

fig. 27
The New Age, London, 19 March 1914, showing *'A Dancer
by Gaudier-Brzeska'*, p. 25, Cambridge University Library

fig. 28
The Sketch, London, 29 October 1913, vol. 84, no. 1083,
showing Alexander Archipenko's *The Dance*, 1912,
Cambridge University Library

fig. 29
Percy Wyndham Lewis (ed.), *BLAST number 1*, London,
1914, Tate

fig. 30
Catalogue for the *Vorticist Exhibition*, Doré Galleries,
London, June – July 1915, cover design by Percy
Wyndham Lewis, Tate

fig. 31
Henri Gaudier-Brzeska, front cover of *20 drawings from
the note-books of H. Gaudier-Brzeska*, Ovid Press,
London, 1919, Cambridge University Library

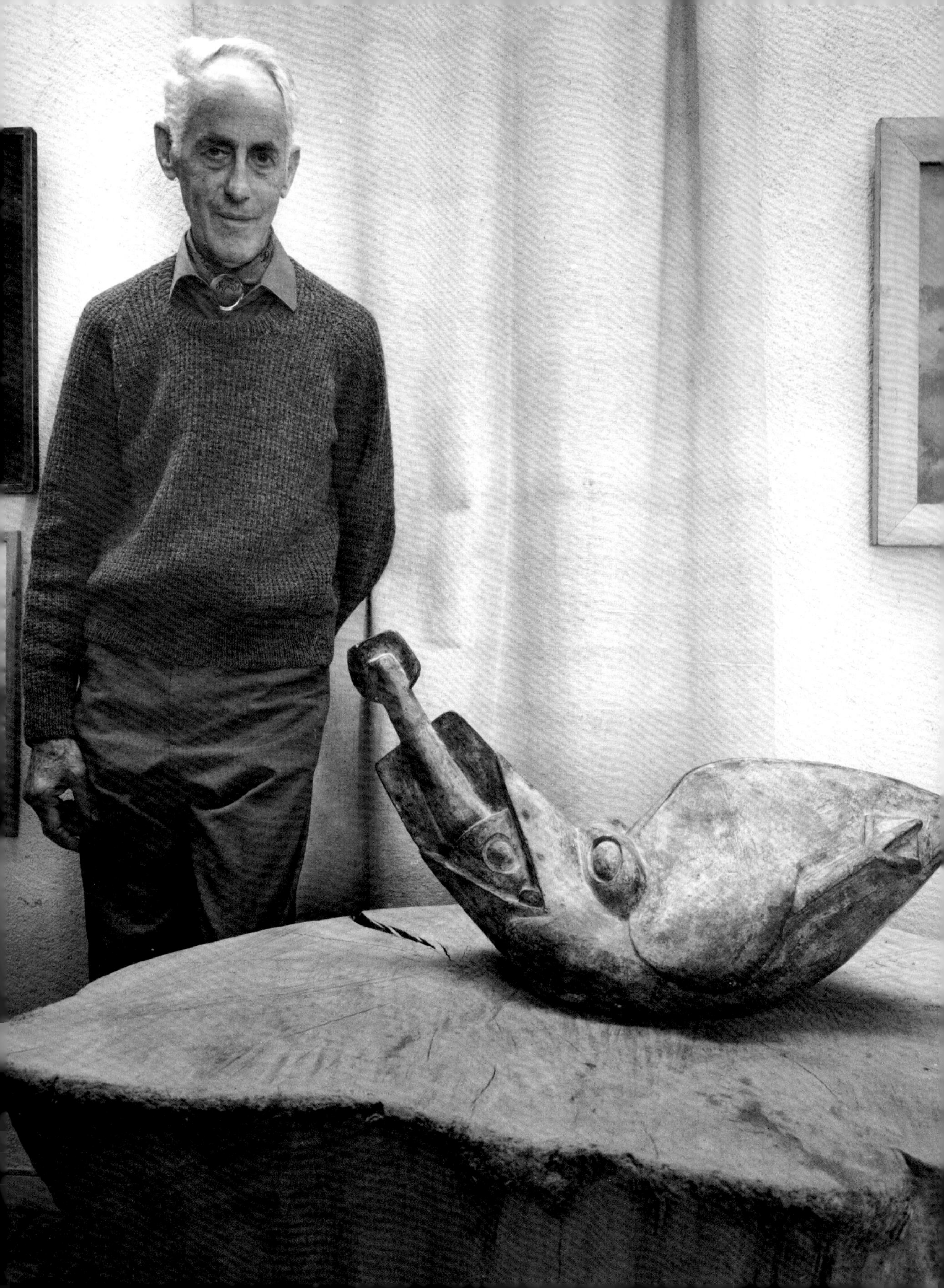

Jim Ede & Henri Gaudier-Brzeska

The founder of Kettle's Yard, Harold Stanley (Jim) Ede and Gaudier both served in the Great War. Gaudier tragically lost his life but Ede returned from the front. Gaudier had bequeathed his estate to Sophie Brzeska in August 1914, but on her death, with no known heir, it passed to the British Treasury who sent it on to the National Gallery, Millbank (Tate) in 1926. Ede was working there as a curator of modern art when crates of Gaudier's drawings, sculptures and papers arrived for his attention.

Ede helped to place three of Gaudier's sculptures (including *Red Stone Dancer*) and seventeen drawings in Tate's collection. They were purchased by Frank Stoop who presented them to the gallery through the Contemporary Art Society. The Society also kept two sculptures and a collection of drawings. Ede recognised Gaudier's precocious talent and offered to purchase the remaining works and papers for £60, about a third of his annual income. Ultimately this was achieved through an intermediary, Ede's friend the artist Edward McKnight Kauffer, who made the purchase on his behalf. In 1927 Ede acquired 19 sculptures, 13 paintings and 1595 drawings by Gaudier. When he opened his home, Kettle's Yard, to the public in 1957, Gaudier's works were displayed at the heart of his extensive collection of twentieth-century art where they can still be viewed today. In the *Cambridge Review* of 1968, Ede proudly described how it was 'possible to come closely into touch with his [Gaudier's] sculpture and indeed to touch it, sensing through the hands a rhythm of planes'. Although these sculptures can no longer be handled for conservation reasons, Kettle's Yard still holds one of the largest collections of the artist's works.

Ede used Gaudier's lively letters to Sophie and his friends, and Sophie's papers as the basis for his memoir on the artist that was published first in a small limited edition as *A Life of Gaudier-Brzeska* (1930), and a year later as *Savage Messiah* in the United States and then in Britain. New York's *World Telegram* described it as 'a book that is going to be the talk of the town' in July 1931. There are nine editions of *Savage Messiah*, the most recent published in 2011 by Kettle's Yard and the Henry Moore Institute; the book indeed continues to fuel intrigue about the artist.

Ede presented works from Gaudier's estate to national museums, and made further bronze and stone casts of numerous original sculptures. Some were patinated in the mid-1960s by the sculptor Henry Moore, who admired *Bird Swallowing a Fish* so much that he asked if he could keep a bronze cast. Sculptures and drawings were donated by Ede to public collections including the Centre Pompidou, Paris, Musée des Beaux-Arts d'Orléans, and the Museum of Fine Arts, Boston. In an interview for the *Smithsonian Magazine* in 1988, he noted that placing Gaudier's work in international collections was not without its challenges, but re-affirmed his unwavering belief that Gaudier may 'one day be recognized as one of France's great sculptors'.

List of works

Henri Gaudier-Brzeska: Sculptures

The Firebird, 1912
Bronze, posthumous cast, n.d., 640 × 325 × 240 mm, By kind permission of the executors of the 7th Earl of Harewood and the Trustees of the Harewood House Trust (pp. 16–17)

The Dancer, 1913
Bronze, posthumous cast 1967, 765 × 220 × 210 mm, Kettle's Yard, University of Cambridge (thereafter KY) (p. 19)

Female torso, 1913
Polyester resin cast of white marble, 1976, 250 × 100 × 80 mm, KY (p. 27)

Red Stone Dancer, c. 1913–14
Red Mansfield stone, 432 × 229 × 229 mm, Tate, Presented by C. Frank Stoop through the Contemporary Art Society 1930 (pp. 20–21)

The Wrestlers tray, 1913
Wood with marquetry, circumference 600 mm, Victoria and Albert Museum, London (p. 103)

Wrestlers relief, c. 1913–14
Posthumous herculite cast, 1965, 725 × 915 mm, KY (p. 109)

Bird Swallowing a Fish, 1914
Plaster, painted, 330 × 580 × 270 mm, KY (p. 113)

Doorknocker, 1914
Cut brass, 178 × 85 × 10 mm, KY (not illustrated)

Henri Gaudier-Brzeska: Works on Paper

Page from Bristol sketchbook, 1909
Graphite on paper, 230 × 140 mm, KY (p. 29)

Black & White poster (aka Boxers), 1911
Gouache on paper, 1020 × 2020 mm, KY (pp. 100–101)

Studies of athletes, 4 sheets, recto/verso, c. 1911
Graphite and black crayon, 250 × 180 mm, St James's Art Books (p. 63)

Bird landing on water, c. 1912–13
Pen and ink on paper, 250 × 185 mm, KY (p. 66)

Girl with skirt blowing, 1912
Black crayon on paper, 250 × 180 mm, KY (p. 64)

Male nude, c. 1912–13
Pen and ink on paper, 380 × 240 mm, KY (p. 99)

Seated figure, c. 1912–13
Graphite on paper, 335 × 200 mm, KY (p. 111)

Seated male nude, c. 1912–13
Pen and ink on paper, 250 × 380 mm, KY (p. 62)

Woman on a horse, c. 1912–13
Pen and ink on paper, 250 × 380 mm, KY (p. 65)

Pik Piçkny Brancusi, c. 1913
Crayon on paper, 360 × 245 mm, KY (not illustrated)

Design for furniture for Roger Fry's Omega Workshops, 1913
Graphite on paper, 260 × 340 mm, The Sherwin Collection, Leeds (p. 104)

Man and woman (Homme et femme), c. 1913–14
Black ink on paper, 500 × 355 mm, gift from the Kettle's Yard Foundation 1965, Centre Pompidou, Musée d'art moderne, Paris (p. 49)

Page from a Chenil Blue Book *Sketch for Red Stone Dancer,* c. 1913–14
Graphite and crayon on paper, 205 × 139 mm, Tate (p. 42)

Self Portrait with a pipe (1), 1913
Graphite on paper, 475 × 310 mm, KY (p. 11)

Self Portrait with a pipe (2), 1913
Pen and Indian ink on paper, 470 × 305 mm, KY (p. 12)

Self Portrait with a pipe (3), 1913
Charcoal on paper, 475 × 310 mm, KY (p. 13)

Two Men Wrestling, c. 1913
Pen and ink on paper, 470 × 352 mm, KY (p. 105)

Two Wrestlers, c. 1913
Graphite on paper, 370 × 250 mm, KY (p. 102)

Dancer (study) (Danseuse (étude)), 1914
Black ink on paper, 385 × 250 mm, Gift from the Kettle's Yard Foundation 1965, Centre Pompidou, Musée d'art moderne, Paris (p. 45)

Dancer on a yellow background (Danseuse sur fond jaune), 1914
Charcoal and watercolour on paper, 480 × 310 mm, Gift from the Kettle's Yard Foundation 1965, Centre Pompidou, Musée d'art moderne, Paris (p. 43)

Female nude, c. 1914
Pen and ink on paper, 370 × 122 mm, KY (p. 47)

Female nude, kneeling and flexing left arm, c. 1914
Indian ink on paper, 215 × 135 mm, KY (p. 110)

Praying Mantis, 1914
Pen and indian ink on paper, 250 × 370 mm, KY (p. 67)

Three Studies for Red Stone Dancer, recto, (Three further Studies, verso), c. 1914
Ink on paper, 165 × 108 mm (each), Jennings Fine Art (p. 46)

Two Wrestlers, 1914
Graphite on paper, 160 × 207 mm, KY (p. 106)

Wrestlers, 1914
Linocut on paper, 225 × 280 mm, KY (p. 107)

Works by other artists

Alexander Archipenko (1887–1964), *The Dance*, 1912–13
Bronze, posthumous cast 1959, 740 × 625 × 375 mm,
Saarlandmuseum Saarbrücken, Stiftung Saarländischer
Kulturbesitz (p. 87)

David Bomberg (1890–1957), *Abstract sketch for
The Dancer,* c. 1913 – 14
Black chalk on paper, 151 × 104 mm, Presented by the
Anthony d'Offay Gallery, The British Museum (not illustrated)

David Bomberg, *Sketch of a figure for The Dancer,* c. 1913–14,
Pen and grey ink; drawn on reverse of a printed calendar,
131 × 158 mm, Presented by the Anthony d'Offay Gallery,
The British Museum (not illustrated)

David Bomberg, *The Dancer,* c. 1913 –14
Oil on canvas, 650 × 460 mm, Private Collection, London (p. 83)

David Bomberg, *The Dancer, abstract design
in red, yellow, brown and blue,* c. 1913 – 14
Watercolour over graphite, 379 × 277 mm, The British Museum,
purchased 1969 (p. 82)

Jacob Epstein, *Nan Seated,* 1910–11
Bronze with a green patina, 515 × 330 × 185 mm, by kind
permission of the executors of the 7th Earl of Harewood
and the Trustees of the Harewood House Trust (p. 58)

Jacob Epstein (1880–1959), *Female Figure in Flenite,* 1913
Serpentine, 457 × 95 × 121 mm, Tate, purchased 1972 (p. 59)

Percy Wyndham Lewis (1882–1957), *The Dancers* (study for
Kermesse), 1912
Watercolour, bodycolour, black ink and pencil on paper,
301 × 292 mm, Manchester City Galleries (p. 86)

William Roberts (1895–1980), *The Toe Dancer*, 1914
Pen and ink and gouache, 666 × 533 mm, Victoria and Albert
Museum, London (p. 79)

William Roberts, *Study for the lost painting Two-Step;
abstract design with orange and green background*, 1915
Graphite, watercolour and gouache, 302 × 228 mm,
The British Museum (p. 81)

William Roberts, *Study for Two Step*, 1915
Graphite on paper, 298 × 229 mm, Tate, purchased 1968 (p. 80)

Auguste Rodin (1840 – 1917), *Dance Movement H (Mouvement
de Danse H),* c. 1911, cast 1950s
Bronze with black marble base, 260 × 294 mm, M.12–2006,
The Fitzwilliam Museum, Cambridge (p. 77)

Auguste Rodin, *Pas-de-Deux, Study type B*, 1911,
posthumous cast 1964
Bronze, height 330 mm, Bowman Sculpture Gallery, London (p. 76)

Auguste Rodin, *Nijinsky,* 1912, posthumous cast 1959
Bronze, height 260 mm, Bowman Sculpture Gallery, London (p. 73)

Helen Saunders (1885 – 1963), *Cabaret,* c. 1913 – 14
Ink and watercolour on paper, 140 × 210 mm, Private Collection
(p. 85)

Helen Saunders, *Vorticist Composition in green or yellow*, c. 1915
Watercolour, bodycolour on paper, 385 × 305 mm, Private
Collection (p. 84)

Contemporary comission

New Rhythms, 2015

Choreographer
Malgorzata Dzierzon

Composer
Kate Whitley

Film Maker
David McCormick

Sound Engineer
Myles Eastwood

Dancers
Estela Merlos and Thomasin Gülgeç

Musicians
Eloisa Fleur Thom and Asher Zaccerdelli

Commissioned by Kettle's Yard

Credits

Copyright

© ADAGP, Paris and DACS, London 2014,
pp. 71, 73, 76–77, 120.

© ARS, NY and DACS, London 2014, p. 87 (fig. 28).

© The Estate of David Bomberg, All Rights Reserved,
DACS 2014, p. 82, 83.

© The Estate of Sir Jacob Epstein, pp. 51, 53, 54, 58, 59.

The Estate of John David Roberts. By permission
of the William Roberts Society, pp. 79, 80, 81.

© The Wyndham Lewis Memorial Trust/
Bridgeman Images, pp. 86, 121, fig. 29.

© The Estate of Helen Saunders, pp. 37, 84, 85.

© Kettle's Yard, University of Cambridge, pp. 10–13, 19, 27, 29,
32, 47, 64, 65, 66, 67, 91, 100–102, 105–107, 109, 110, 111, 113.

Photography

Albert Sloman Library, University of Essex, pp. 22, 93.
Courtesy Archive of Modern Conflict, pp. 7, 23, 127.
© Bristol Museums, Galleries & Archives, p. 97.
Courtesy of Bowman Sculpture Gallery, London, pp. 73, 76.
Photograph © Christie's Images/ Bridgeman Images, p. 46.
© Fitzwilliam Museum, University of Cambridge, p. 77.
Jennings Fine Art, p. 46.
Reproduced by the kind permission of the Executors of the
7th Earl of Harewood and the Trustees of the Harewood House
Trust, pp. 16, 17, 58.
Leeds Museums and Galleries (Henry Moore Institute Archive),
p. 51.
Photography Andy Keate, p. 63.
© Manchester City Galleries, p. 86.
Modernist Journals Project www.modjourn.org, p. 120 (fig. 27).
© Musée Historique et Archéologique de l'Orléanais, Orléans/
photograph François Lauginie, p. 26.
Photograph © 2015, Museum of Fine Arts, Boston, p. 30.
© National Portrait Gallery, London, p. 25.
Photograph © Centre Pompidou, MNAM–CCI, Dist. RMN–Grand
Palais/Droits réservés, pp. 43, 49.
Photograph © Centre Pompidou, MNAM–CCI, Dist. RMN–Grand
Palais/Bertrand Prévost, p. 71.
Photograph © Centre Pompidou, MNAM–CCI, Dist. RMN–Grand
Palais/Adam Rzepka, p. 45.
Photograph © Centre Pompidou, MNAM–CCI, Dist. RMN–Grand
Palais/Francois Vizzavona/reproduction RMN, p. 74.
Private Collection, California, pp. 53, 54.
Private Collection, London, p. 83.
Private Collection, pp. 84, 85.
Saarlandmuseum Saarbrücken, Stiftung Saarländischer
Kulturbesitz, p. 87.
The Sherwin Collection, Leeds, UK/Bridgeman images,
pp. 95, 104.
Courtesy of The David and Alfred Smart Museum of Art,
The University of Chicago, p. 37.
Courtesy St James's Art Books, London, p. 63.
By permission of the Syndics of Cambridge University Library,
pp. 31, 36, 121 (figs. 26, 28, 31).
© Tate, London 2014/15, pp. 9, 18, 20–21, 42, 59, 80, 121 (fig. 29).
© The Trustees of the British Museum, pp. 81, 82.
© Victoria and Albert Museum, London, pp. 79, 103, 121 (fig. 30).
Photography Simon Warner, pp. 16–17.
© Kettle's Yard, University of Cambridge, photography
Paul Allitt, pp. 10, 29, 32, 34, 120 (figs. 23, 24, 25).

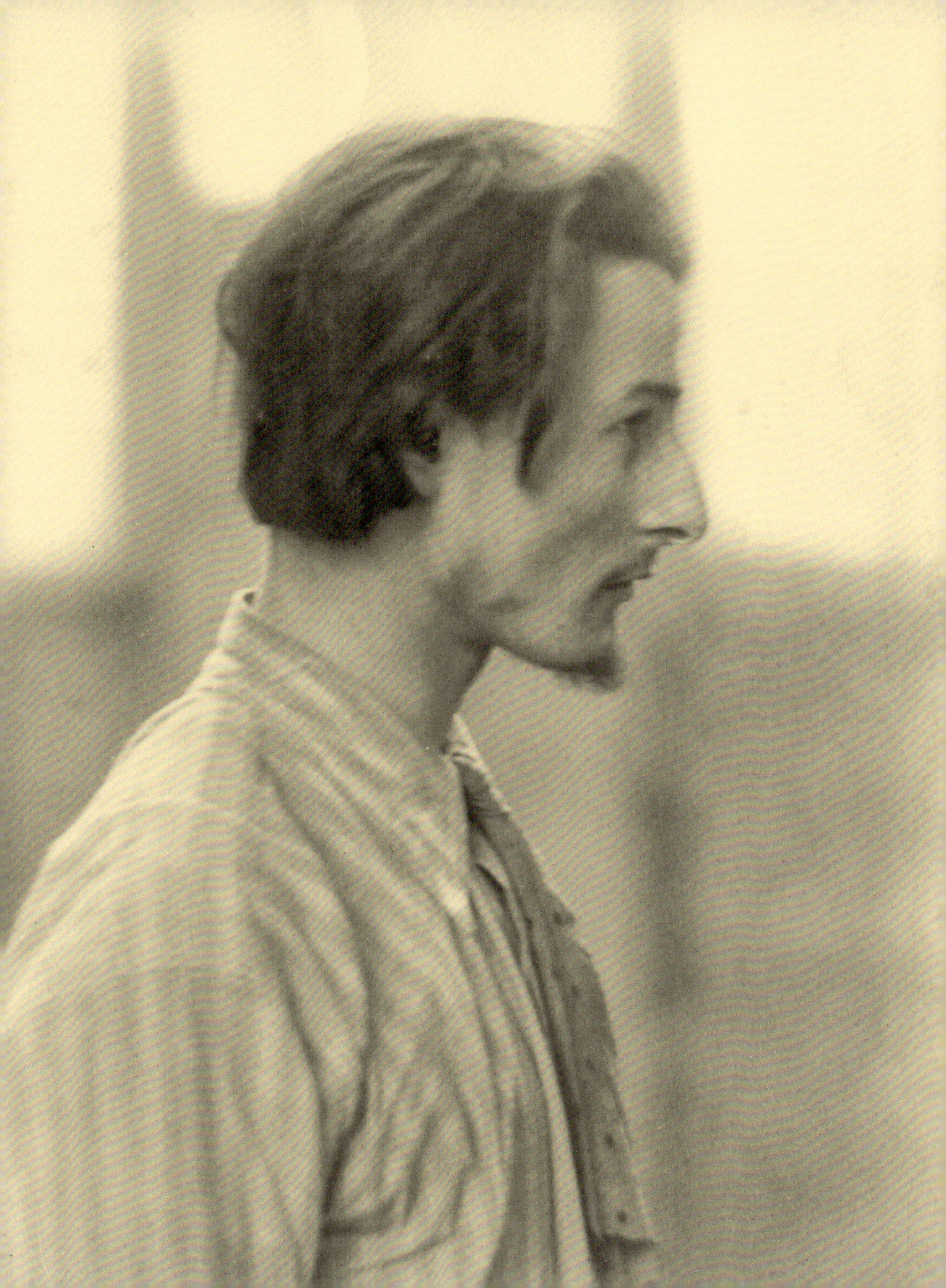

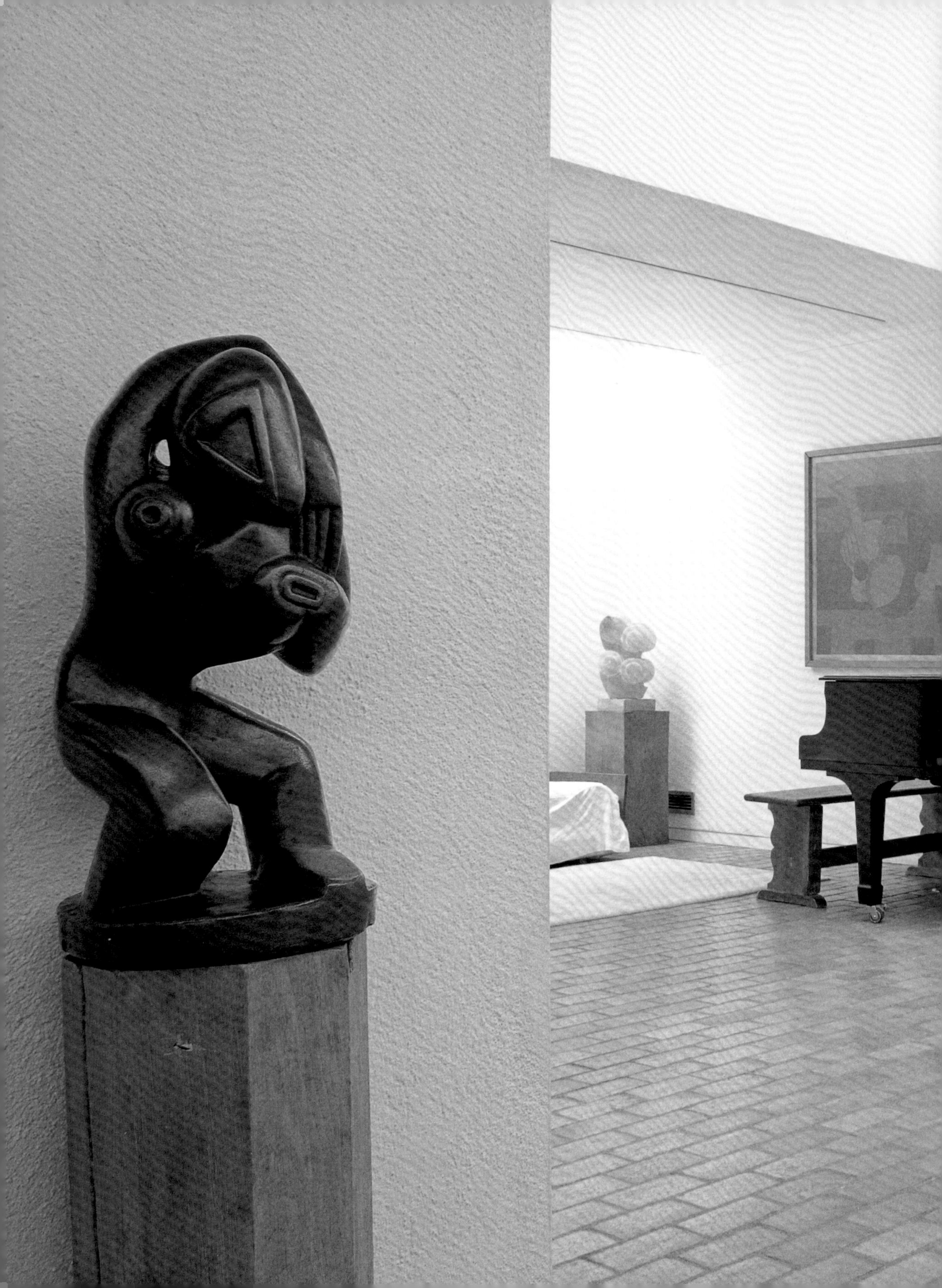